THE
BEADER'S
HANDBOOK

THE
BEADER'S
HANDBOOK

Beads • Tools • Materials • Techniques

Juju Vail

Martingale®
& COMPANY

An Hachette Livre UK Company

First published in Great Britain in 2007
by Hamlyn, a division of Octopus Publishing
Group Ltd, 2–4 Heron Quays, London E14 4JP
www.octopusbooks.co.uk

Martingale & Company
20205 144th Ave. NE
Woodinville, WA 98072-8478 USA
www.martingale-pub.com

Martingale®
& C O M P A N Y

12 11 10 09 08 07   6 5 4 3 2 1

Library of Congress Cataloging-in-Publication
Data is available.

ISBN: 978-1-56477-800-0

Mission Statement
Dedicated to providing quality products
and service to inspire creativity.

*To David, for keeping my "whim of iron" in
check. And to my fellow blog readers and writers
for including me in the great online worldwide
craft community. "More Pie!"*

contents

INTRODUCTION

This book can be read from beginning to end to get an overview of beading techniques or it can be dipped into as a reference when needed. The chapters are arranged by topics and techniques that should make finding the information you are looking for easy. Clear photographs of tools, materials, and beads provide a quick visual reference for items when you are uncertain of their names.

a guide to beading

Beading is an absorbing hobby. You need very little equipment and the materials are a joy to collect and will provide much of the inspiration for your pieces. In addition, beads are portable and do not require much storage or work space.

It is a pleasure to quickly make up a piece of jewelry to complement an outfit, or create a pair of earrings as a gift. Embarking on a larger project is also exciting, because the beauty and colors of the beads reveal themselves as you work.

Whether you're completely new to beading or an experienced beader who needs an occasional reminder or wants to add an unfamiliar technique to your repertoire, you will find this book invaluable.

It will guide you in completing your first beading projects by offering step-by-step instructions for all beading techniques and complete photographic references for all the essentials that you need.

The Tools and Equipment section offers excellent photographic references to help you tell your needle-nose pliers from your flat-nose pliers, and your crimps from your bead tips.

The Bead Basics section will guide you in stringing beads and finishing them with different kinds of clasps and findings. It also explains the main types of adhesives and when to use them. Additionally, it offers several different techniques for making beads at home. These will greatly increase your jewelry design possibilities.

Working with Wire describes all the cold-working wire methods. This means forming wire without the use of heat and solder. From these fundamental techniques, infinite variations are possible. Beautiful jewelry can be made with only beads and wire, or wire may be worked to create a variety of unique findings for your beadwork.

The Stitching and Weaving section demonstrates the most popular methods for working with beads. These include knotting, weaving on and off a loom, embroidery, knitting, and crocheting.

This book features a unique bead directory, richly illustrated with photographs. This explains the differences between similar beads and offers a great reference to the variety of cuts, shapes, and finishes available on the market. This is crucial for the beader who may be ordering materials over the Internet or who becomes overwhelmed by the choices in the local bead shop.

Finally, graphs are provided for the most popular bead-weaving stitches. These can be photocopied and colored to help plan your own designs. Within this book you will find all the information and help you need to create beautiful beadwork. Enjoy beading!

TOOLS AND EQUIPMENT

Many people adopt beading as a hobby because it requires so few tools. String or thread, scissors, and beads are the only essentials. However, as your interest increases and you explore new techniques, you will need to acquire more tools and materials. This chapter guides you in choosing the best tools and equipment that are suitable for the job.

basic tools

The following is a list of the basic tools you will need for beading. These items are inexpensive and worth equipping yourself with, no matter which technique you pursue. It is advisable to have a set of specific bead needles since they may be used to finish off other projects. They are easily obtained from beading suppliers.

small sharp scissors

You will need a good pair of scissors to trim threads close to your beading work. Nail scissors are very good for this purpose. Select a pair with a straight edge.

white and dark flannel cloths

Working on a cloth rather than directly on the tabletop prevents the beads from rolling around. Lay piles of seed beads on the cloth and use a teaspoon to scoop leftover beads back into their containers. Choose a white cloth for most beading work. Use a black cloth when you are working with mostly white beads.

small clamps or clips

When you are not working on a strand, it is essential to clamp it in order to secure the beads. You can use stationery clips, clothespins, or small clips found in electronics shops, but be sure to choose ones with no teeth so you do not damage the beading cords.

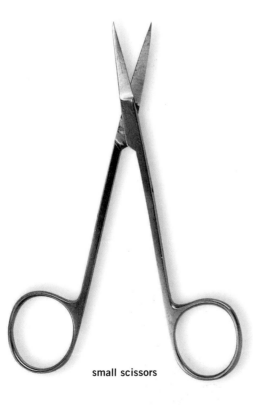

small scissors

small stationery clips

t-pin

A T-pin is just like a straight dressmaker's pin but with a bar on top instead of a round or oval head. It is useful for knotting thread close to a bead hole because the knot will not come off.

stopper bead

This is not strictly a piece of equipment, but is useful nonetheless. A stopper bead is an ordinary bead that prevents beads falling off the thread when there is no knot. It also helps to maintain tension while you are working. Use a bead in a different color so that you remember to remove it when the work is complete. Bring your needle through the stopper bead and back around through the same side again. Begin your work.

good lighting

It is essential to be able to see clearly the tiny beads and the eye in the needle. Work in a bright area with no shadows. To avoid shadows, place light directly above the work surface or use two lights, one in front of you and another above you.

clear plastic ruler and measuring tape

You'll need these to measure thread and strands of beads while you are working. A clear plastic ruler is particularly useful for counting bead-woven rows accurately through the plastic. Some rulers also have magnifying inserts.

plastic ruler

measuring tape

beading needles

Available in several sizes, beading needles are longer and more flexible than dressmaker's needles. They are useful for loom-weaving beadwork, some off-loom techniques, beading fringes, and when stringing necklaces with nylon thread.

sharps needles

These are shorter and more rigid than beading needles. They are great for beading beads and buttons. The higher the needle-size number, the finer the needle. Fine needles break easily, so always have extras on hand. Needle size 12 is suitable for bead sizes 10° to 14°. Needle size 13 is suitable for bead sizes 10° to 15°. Needle sizes 15 and 16 are suitable for beads smaller than 14°.

twisted wire needles

These have a large eye so they are easier to thread than Sharps and beading needles. However, they are not as rigid, which can make weaving with them more difficult.

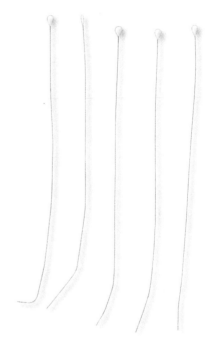

beading needles

sharps needles

twisted wire needles

beeswax

Wax is used to condition nylon threads. It makes the thread stronger, easier to maintain a firm tension, and less likely to become tangled. It is best used when working with a doubled thread as it helps the two ends stick together. After threading the needle, run the thread through the wax and then through your fingers to remove excess wax.

thread conditioner

Synthetic thread conditioner is available as an alternative to beeswax. It prevents the thread ends from sticking to one another and becoming tangled. Use it in the same manner as wax when working with a single thread.

thread conditioner

beeswax

bead reamer

These enlarge stone and pearl holes when you need to fit two threads through. You can buy electric bead reamers, but a simple manual one is fine for occasional use.

bead reamer

wirework tools

The tools on these pages are specifically required for working cold-wire techniques. It is not necessary to begin by owning them all. However, all beaders should own one good pair of needle-nose pliers and one pair of round-nose pliers as well as a pair of wire cutters. These are essential parts of the beader's kit.

anvils or bench blocks

Anvils and bench blocks are small metal blocks, which you place underneath wire or metal to flatten or reshape it. For most wire work, a small 2³/8 in (6 cm) square bench block is adequate.

flush cutters

These are essential for the trimming of eyepins, headpins, and beading wire to result in perfectly flush ends. Flush cutters come in several sizes, depending on the size of wire to be trimmed.

anvils or bench blocks

flush cutters

chain-nose pliers

Chain-nose pliers are a good all-purpose tool for beading. They are particularly useful for gripping chain links to close them. Needle-nose pliers are also useful for this purpose but chain-nose pliers have a more robust tip.

round-nose pliers

Used for bending wire into small loops. Choose a pair with variation in diameter from the tip to the base of the jaw so that you can select which circumference to use to make your loops.

needle-nose pliers

These pliers are useful for gently coaxing needles through beads filled with thread as well as for bending wires when attaching clasps or jump rings, for example. Buy the best pair you can afford. The best quality pliers will have tips that meet perfectly.

round-nose pliers

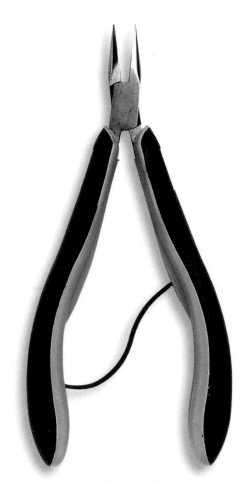

needle-nose pliers

crimping pliers

These specialist pliers curl and flatten crimp beads. Flat-nose pliers will flatten crimp beads adequately, but crimping pliers curve the bead, making it smoother for the wearer.

flat-nose pliers

Flat-nose pliers are completely flat on their inside edge; they do not come to a point at the tip the way needle-nose pliers do. They are particularly useful for grabbing wire, because they have a large surface area and make a good, all-purpose tool. They come in many nose widths.

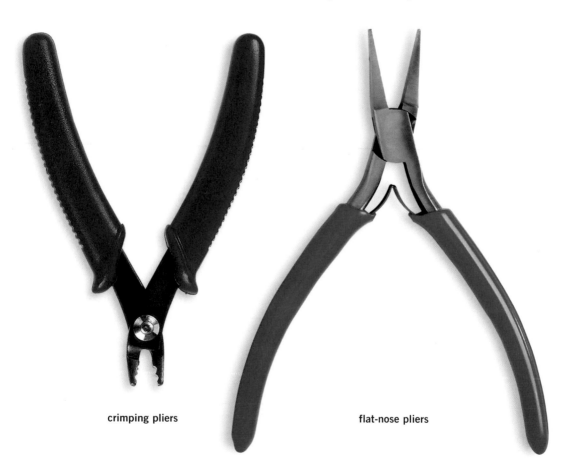

crimping pliers   **flat-nose pliers**

wire jigs

Wire jigs are extremely useful for bending wire into an assortment of shapes. The basic design of a jig resembles a pegboard; the wire is wrapped around the pegs to bend it. Some models have stationary pegs, but others are designed to allow the pegs to be removed and rearranged into different patterns. The best wire-jig models have a durable transparent plastic base with metal pegs.

The transparent base allows you to see a design underneath it, while the metal pegs are more durable. Your choice of jig size will depend on the gauge of wire you intend to use.

files

A set of jeweler's needle files is a necessity for getting rid of snags and burrs at wire ends. The most useful file has a flat edge and pointed tip. Files are often sold in packs of assorted shapes.

steel wool

Fine-grade steel wool is used to polish and smooth the finished surface of metal. It is used after all snags and burrs have been removed with a file but before a polishing cloth is used to buff the surface to a shine.

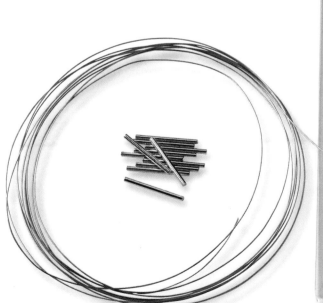

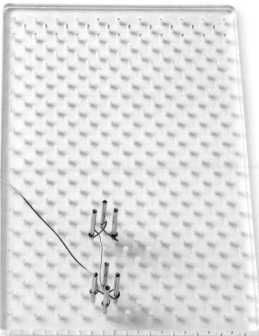

transparent wire jig

chasing hammer

Metal hammers are used for flattening objects and making decorative designs. The wide, flat end is used for flattening wire and striking chasing tools, while the round end is for riveting and for making decorative designs on metals.

polishing cloth

Polishing cloths are used to remove tarnish and restore luster in metals. Polishing with the cloth is the final process involved in working with silver or other metal wires.

rubber or plastic mallet

Rubber- or plastic-headed mallets are used for striking the wire without making a dent. This is useful when hardening or straightening wire or setting a shape.

mandrel

Mandrels are used to make a series of consistent round shapes in wire. Pencils, dowels, knitting needles, and bamboo skewers all make good mandrels. They can also be purchased from jewelry suppliers in a variety of sizes, including one for rings that increases in circumference for different ring sizes.

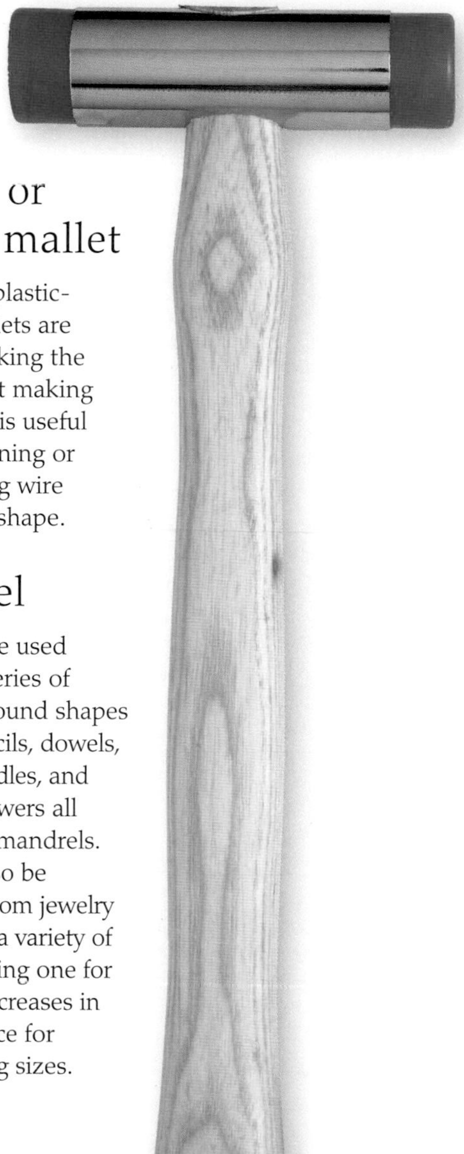

chasing hammer

plastic mallet

other tools

The following tools are useful if you intend to try specific techniques, such as loom weaving or bead knitting, but are not essential. However, most of these tools are inexpensive and are worth having on hand so that you are prepared for any beading possibility.

bead-weaving loom

A number of different bead-weaving looms are available, including simple ones for making bracelets. These are good to start with as they are inexpensive and perfectly adequate for small projects. If you decide to do a lot of bead weaving, you may like to construct your own loom or buy a larger one. Looms are available as vertical models, or those which lie flat on a tabletop; this is a matter of personal choice.

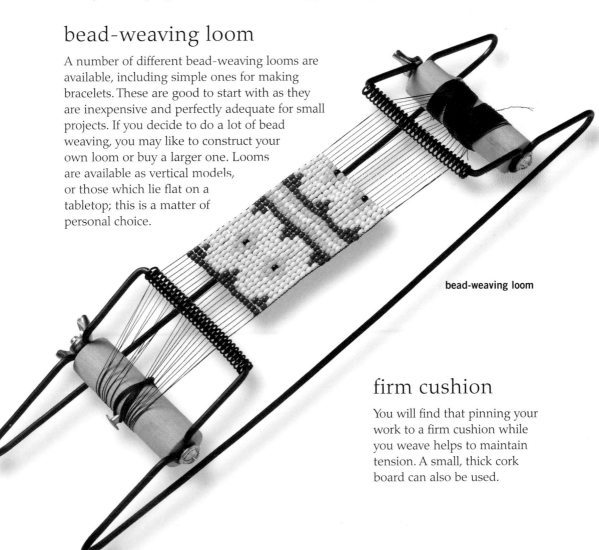

bead-weaving loom

firm cushion

You will find that pinning your work to a firm cushion while you weave helps to maintain tension. A small, thick cork board can also be used.

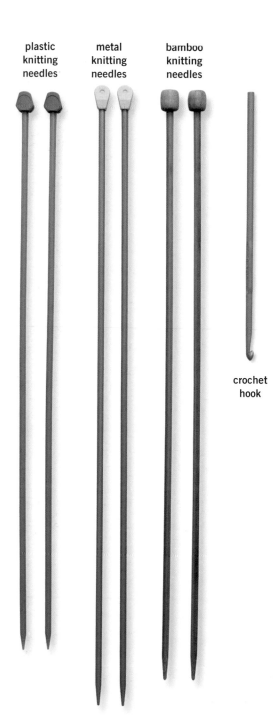

plastic
knitting
needles

metal
knitting
needles

bamboo
knitting
needles

crochet
hook

knitting needles

Knitting needles can be used as mandrels as well as for knitting yarn with strung beads. An assortment of sizes is useful. Mandrels are used to wrap wire to create perfectly even-shaped rings and jump rings.

crochet hooks

Crochet hooks are used for crocheting yarn strung with beads. In most cases, the smallest sizes are the most useful. Larger sizes are good if you plan to crochet thicker yarns embellished with beads.

necklace-planning board

There are a few different types of bead board, but most will have at least one long groove around the board to set the beads as you prepare to string. On either side of this groove are measurements to help you determine the final length of a piece of beaded jewelry. In the center of the board are extra compartments to store beads as you work. Some bead boards have more than one groove, which can be useful for making multistranded items.

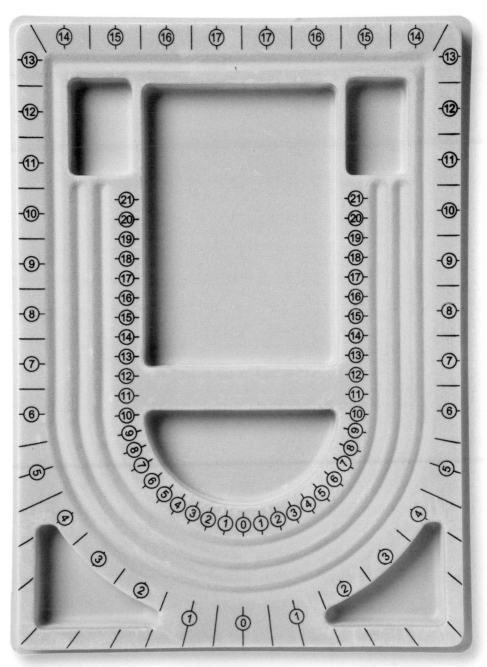

necklace-planning board

threads and cords

Threads and cords are an essential part of a beader's kit. Often there is more than one type that may be suitable for a project and the selection will be a matter of personal preference. Familiarize yourself with the different options, learn their strengths and draping qualities.

fishing line

Many jewelry projects can be strung on fishing line. While it does not drape as nicely as silk or beading wire, it is very strong. It can be bought on a spool in clear or with a slight blue tint, which makes it easier to see. A reel of 12 lb (5.4 kg) test-weight fishing line (also called monofilament) lasts a long time and is extremely economical. It fits through many beads and because it is stiff does not require a needle. The ends are knotted and woven back through beads.

nylon beading thread

Used with lightweight beads such as seed beads, and for stringing light necklaces as well as weaving. Nylon beading thread is strong and drapes well. It comes in many colors and various sizes. The smallest size is 00, ideal for beads size 16° and smaller. Size 0 is for beads 14° and smaller, size B is for beads between 11° and 15°, and size D is for beads between 6° and 12°. Be aware that some older glass beads and some metal beads have sharp edges that may cut nylon threads over time. Use beading wire or fishing line for these.

nylon beading thread

fishing line

silk cord

Silk cords can be bought with an already attached needle, in a variety of sizes and colors. Thread made from twisted strands of silk is traditionally used for stringing pearls and light gems. Silk is said to have the best drape of any fiber.

elastic

Beading elastic is available in a range of sizes and colors, including clear. It is useful for stringing a stretchy string of beads, which can fit over a wrist. Making bracelets with elastic beading string avoids the need for a closure. Use a square knot to fasten the two ends of the elastic and secure with a drop of super glue.

beading wire

There are several brands of beading wire available. It is made of many tiny wire filaments wrapped in a smooth coating. It is strong, drapes nicely, and comes in many colors and finishes. A crimp bead is crushed around it to finish the work because it does not knot. It is a good alternative to fishing line but can be costly.

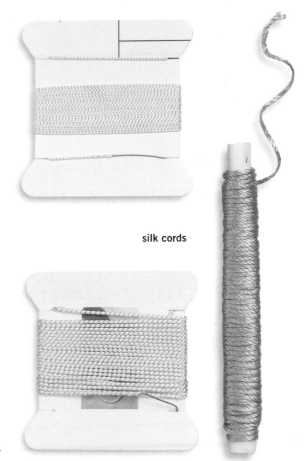

silk cords

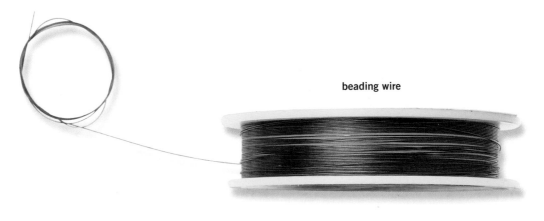

beading wire

cords of nylon, rubber, and leather

These come in many sizes and colors, and are often used to hang a pendant. They can also be used in strung and knotted necklaces. They require beads with larger holes. Test the hole size before you thread the entire necklace.

satin cord or rattail

Satin cord or rattail is a satiny cord available in a wide range of colors and several widths. It is commonly used in Chinese knotting and different braiding techniques. It is easy to knot as the satiny material makes it slippery. Beads and decorative knots can be combined on rattail to make beautiful jewelry.

satin rattail

leather cord

linen beading thread

Linen thread holds knots well and is useful for necklaces that include macramé knotting. Some linen threads come waxed to provide a good grip for knotting.

nylon cord

linen beading thread

findings

Findings are the many different metal pieces used for attaching jewelry parts together and to the body. Some of them make great features in themselves. Although most of the illustrations here show sterling silver findings, most are available in a wide variety of base and precious metals.

chain

Ready-made chain can be bought in a huge variety of styles and metals, by the foot or meter. Beads and findings can be attached to the chain with jump rings.

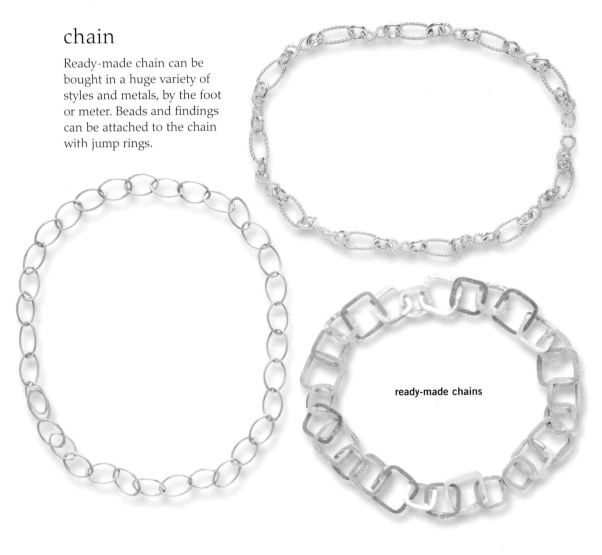

ready-made chains

headpins and eyepins

Used to make bead dangles, especially earrings. They also come in a variety of metals. Choose one to suit the color of your beads.

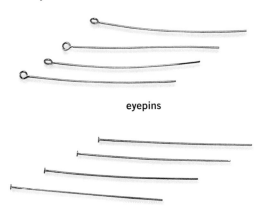

eyepins

headpins

hook-and-eye crimp clasps

Crimp ends, or leather crimps, are specially designed to attach the end of leather, satin, or linen cord to a finding without using knots. Sometimes they include the finding in the crimp.

hook-and-eye crimp clasps

crimp beads

These are soft metal beads that are crushed around beading wire in place of knots to secure beads in place. They come in a variety of metal finishes.

crimp beads

crimp bead covers

These can be used to conceal crimp beads and add a polished look to your jewelry. They fit over the crimp beads and are closed with two pairs of pliers the same way you close split rings.

cones and end caps

Cones and end caps are used to conceal the area where a string of beads is attached to the finding. They are most commonly used to gather a number of strands together onto one finding. They provide a decorative, professional finish.

spacers

Spacers can be any thin beads. They are useful for making space between beads so that the necklace articulates better. They can also be used to conceal joins in small areas. The spacers illustrated here are also often used in long clusters on their own.

cones   **end caps**

spacers

clamshell bead tips

These are also called bead tips and knot cups. Shaped like a clam, these bead tips conceal knots and crimp beads at the ends of strands.

bead caps

Bead caps are used to create a decorative end on a bead. They hide large holes and make a professional finish, which can be useful when stringing a handmade bead.

clamshell bead tips

bead caps

multi-hole spacer bars

Multi-hole spacer bars are great for multi-strand necklaces or bracelets. They hold the strands at pleasing intervals apart from one another. They can also be used to make a change in the number of strands within a necklace.

closures

These include lobster clasps, spring rings, hooks and eyes, S-clasps, toggles, barrels, fish hooks, pearl closures, and magnetic clasps. Used for fastening necklaces and bracelets, they are available in many styles and sizes.

spacer bars

closures

multi-row fasteners

Multi-row fasteners have multiple rings to fasten jewelry with many strands. Not every loop needs to be used if the beads are very large. They provide a professional way of finishing multi-strand jewelry.

multi-row fasteners

brooch backs

A variety of brooch backs are available. Some are designed to be visible and decorative with loops to attach beads; others are very simple and are meant to be sewn to the back of jewelry. Right-handed people prefer to undo a clasp on the left side of the brooch. Test the clasp to make sure that it operates properly.

earring wires and earring posts

These come in silver, gold, plated, brass, and surgical-steel styles. It is advisable to avoid the brass and plated ones because they can cause ear infections. Use the best you can afford.

screw or clip ear findings

If you plan to make earrings for people without pierced ears, you will need screw or clip ear findings. These are still available, although becoming less common, at bead-supply stores.

split rings

These rings attach one part of a piece of jewelry to another. They have a split in the ring to open and close them. They can easily be made at home with the help of a mandrel.

earring posts

earring backs

split rings

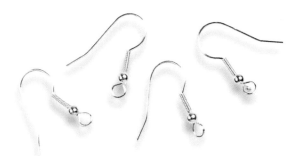

earring wires

wires

Some experience with cold wireworking is essential to make earrings, dangles, and clasps for beaded jewelry. Cold wirework refers to any wireworking techniques that do not involve solder or heat; these include cutting, wrapping, and hammering. Developing these techniques further allows a beader to complete intricate silver, brass, copper, or gold pieces.

wire gauge

A wire's size is determined by its diameter. In North America, wire size is measured in gauge (AWG); the smaller the gauge number, the thicker the wire. In most European countries, wire size is measured in millimeters. The chart (opposite) shows American wire-gauge sizes with their metric equivalents. Sometimes when wire is sold in Europe, the diameter size is rounded off; the most commonly used rounded-off measurements have been included in brackets.

shape

Wire is available in a variety of different cross sections, such as round, half-round, triangular, and square.

Round is the most common and versatile and is recommended for the beginner. It can be used to create jump rings, clasps, and earring hooks.

Half-round is used for rings where the shape of the wire fits more comfortably against the finger. Other shapes are worth experimenting with once you have gained confidence in the basic techniques.

hardness

Wire is usually sold in four different levels of hardness: dead soft, soft, half-hard, and full-hard.

Dead-soft wire is very soft and can be bent with your hands. It is often used for making wire-wrapped jewelry with thicker gauges.

Soft wire When dead soft is not available, soft wire makes a suitable substitute in most gauge sizes.

Half-hard wire is very versatile. It is soft enough to bend, yet strong enough to act as a functional component in jewelry. This wire is suitable for ear hooks, eyepins, and closures.

Full-hard wire is obviously harder than half-hard and is very strong, but it is also trickier to work with. It is suitable for functional components of jewelry and cold-worked chain techniques.

wire size chart

Diameter of wire (mm)	American wire gauge (AWG) size
7.348	1
6.544	2
5.827	3
5.189	4
4.621	5
4.115	6
3.665	7
3.264	8
2.906	9
2.588	10
2.305	11
2.053	12
1.828	13
1.628	14
1.450	15
1.291	16
1.150	17
1.024 (1 mm)	18
0.9116	19
0.8118 (.8 mm)	20
0.7229	21
0.6438 (.6 mm)	22
0.5733	23
0.5106 (.5 mm)	24
0.4547	25
0.4049 (.4 mm)	26
0.3606	27
0.3211 (.3 mm)	28
0.2859	29
0.2546 (.25 mm)	30
0.2268	31
0.2019 (.2 mm)	32
0.1798	33
0.1601	34
0.1426	35
0.1270	36

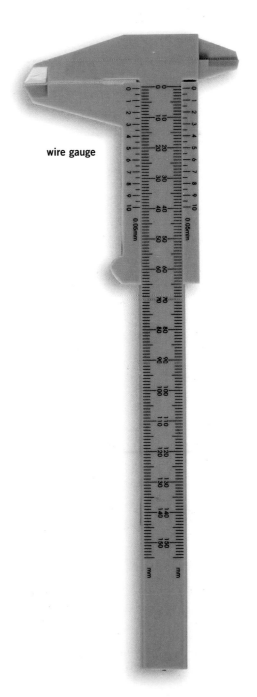

wire gauge

types of wire

Sterling silver and fine silver wire
Sterling silver indicates that the wire is 92.5% pure silver. The rest is made up of metal alloys to provide strength. Sterling will tarnish (oxidize) in time, but can be polished to return it to its bright silver state. Fine silver is made up of 99.9% pure silver. It is softer than sterling, and because it has fewer alloys, it does not tarnish as quickly.

Galvanized wire is a dull silver color and is available in most hardware stores. It is suitable for practice but is much harder than silver wire, so choose thinner gauges.

Brass wire is a yellow-gold color and is available in a variety of gauges and levels of hardness.

Copper wire is good to use as a practice wire because it is inexpensive and easy to manipulate. It can be used to make finished jewelry as well, but be aware that it will darken and discolor with age (the resulting finish is called a patina). You can polish it if you prefer to keep it a bright pink-gold color. It is available in a wide range of gauges.

Gold and gold-filled wire Gold wire is available in various carats (from 10 to 24) and different colors, such as rose gold and white gold. It is very soft and easy to work with, although expensive. If you like the look of it but find it too expensive, try gold-filled wire, which is cheaper and long lasting.

brass wire

gold wire

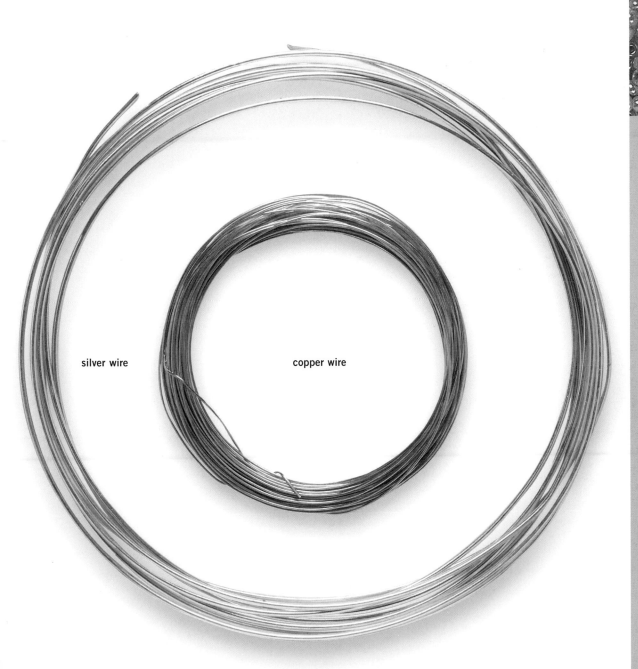

silver wire

copper wire

TOOLS AND EQUIPMENT

Memory wire is a thin, tempered, stainless steel wire. It is usually resistant to corrosion and tarnishing. Like a spring, memory wire is rigid and snaps back to its original form when expanded and released. The wire "remembers" its shape and retains its coil form. It comes in circumferences suitable for necklaces, bracelets, rings, and wine-glass tags, and is available in gold and silver tones in a number of different diameters.

Colored wire has become very popular and is available in many colors and gauges. Keep in mind that the wire is only coated with color, and it can mark easily if scratched with metal tools. Wrap pliers in masking tape to avoid scratches. It is suitable for making items where the wire is covered with beads, such as beaded flowers and other ornaments.

Niobium wire is a silver-colored metal that is anodized to create a thin colored film on the surface. It is available in pink, purple, dark blue, teal, green, and gold. It is strong, corrosion-resistant, and totally hypoallergenic. The coating is resistant enough for niobium wire to be used in most types of jewelry, but it is not indestructible. Take care not to stretch the wire because the color will thin and become grayish. Also, wrap plier tips in masking tape when working with niobium to prevent scratches and nicks. Niobium that is sold for jewelry making is processed to be half-hard. It can be used for cold-process chain making and, although more difficult than gold or silver, can also be used for jump rings and pins.

memory wire

colored wire

glues and adhesives

Glues and adhesives are an essential part of a beader's techniques and tools. They can be used to create strong bonds between beads and a surface as well as for attaching metal components. The secret lies in knowing which adhesive to choose for an application. Additionally, glues can strengthen other beading techniques, such as knotting.

instant and super glues

Instant or super glues are used to reconnect common materials (such as a broken bead) or bond different materials. They are good for general repairs or bonding of most surfaces and provide instant adhesion. They also expand as they cure, filling any gaps in joints. For long-term use, epoxy is preferable, but instant glues can be used to position a piece of jewelry before an epoxy is used to set the item. Instant glues can also be used to stop thread ends from unraveling. Always follow the manufacturer's instructions and safety precautions.

super tacky white glue

Choose a brand that states that it dries clear and is flexible as well as featuring excellent "grab." The flexibility inherent in these glues will prevent beads from cracking off a movable surface, such as fabric. Therefore, these glues are useful for bonding porous items, such as adhering beads or sequins to fabric. They can also be used to stick embellishments, such as sequins, to beads and buttons.

epoxy glue

A two-part epoxy is used for bonding nonporous materials, such as two metal parts. An example would be gluing a metal earring back to a flat glass bead. The two parts (a resin and a catalyst) are combined to create a chemical reaction. This reaction quickly forms a bond. Most epoxies begin to set within five minutes, but some brands are quicker. The bond is extremely strong and resists almost anything, from water to solvents. However, use caution, because epoxy glue is toxic and flammable. Follow the manufacturer's directions and safety precautions.

clear nail polish or fray preventer

These are mostly used to prevent thread ends from unraveling and to strengthen important knots. A little touch of clear nail polish will harden the ends of threads, making them easy to trim and conceal.

BEAD BASICS

This chapter includes the most basic
stringing techniques needed to make beaded
jewelry. It guides you in selecting the best
length and the stringing materials you will
need, as well as how to choose and use your
fastenings and findings.

jewelry length

Although there are standard lengths for necklaces, bracelets, and earrings, these will vary with the individual. A small change can dramatically alter the style, so audition jewelry on the body before finishing it.

To decide how long to make a piece of jewelry, copy the length of an existing piece. If the weight of the new piece is very different, however, you'll need to consider the following: a necklace that has a pendant or heavier beads at the front will hang lower and form a V-shape; a bracelet or necklace made with large beads will need extra length since the inner circumference will be smaller.

necklaces

Choker Worn at the throat, a choker is usually about 15 in (37.5 cm), depending on neck size. It must have a closure.

Princess A princess is 18 in (45 cm) long. It must have a closure.

Matinee A matinee is 20–24 in (50–60 cm). Make it with a closure since hairstyles can make it difficult to put the necklace on over the head.

Opera An opera is 28–30 in (70–75 cm). It is worn as a single strand with or without a closure.

Lariat or rope This is 45 in (112.5 cm) or longer. It can be worn as a single strand or wrapped around the neck more than once. A closure is not necessary.

Ask yourself the following questions when deciding how long to make a necklace:

• What will the necklace be worn with?
• Is it meant to hang within the frame of a garment neckline or outside a shirt or collar? Measure the neckline of a garment on the body to be sure the necklace sits inside or out.
• How will the wearer's body shape affect the way the necklace hangs? Sometimes necklaces get bunched up between ample bosoms or forced under the armpits.

bracelets

To determine the length of beading for a bracelet with a closure, measure the circumference of the wrist and add $9/16$ in (1.5 cm). Determine the total length of the closure system (include the fastener, bead tips, crimps, and other components), and subtract this from your first measurement to give the length of beading required. For a looser fit, make sure it doesn't have more than a thumb's width of slack or it could slip off the hand and be lost.

tip
Consider using an adjustable fastener on a bracelet, especially if you don't know who will wear it. Wrists can vary a lot in size.

pearl stringing with knots

Pearl knots are the small knots between beads on a traditional pearl necklace. They can be useful with many sorts of beads because they help to create articulation and a fine finish to a necklace or bracelet.

Pearl knots can be used with other sorts of beads, but because the knots can be tiny, you may need to double up on your thread or cord, or choose a thicker one if your beads have large holes. It is difficult to combine beads with a variety of hole sizes on the same strand, since a thicker cord will not thread through the smaller beads. A pearl knot is made after threading a bead. Make a loose overhand knot (see page 88). Insert a pin through the knot into the bead hole and tighten, using the pin to ensure the knot lies right next to the bead.

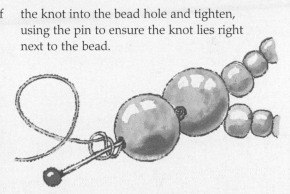

starting and ending threads

Jewelry construction is most vulnerable at the areas of joins and openings. For this reason, great attention should be paid to how thread and cord ends are finished and begun. Bead weaving will usually necessitate a number of different thread ends. Here is how to begin and finish them professionally.

beginning a new thread

When beginning a new thread, always leave a 4 in (10 cm) tail to work into the beading later. If you are beginning a new thread partway through the work, weave it in and out of a few beads before you begin adding new beads so that you have a secure end against which to work. This will give even tension over the whole of your work.

weaving in ends

Whenever you have finished a piece of bead weaving or a necklace strand, you don't want to trim the thread ends too close to the knot, or the knot may come undone. To avoid this problem, weave the thread ends back through the last few beads (see below).

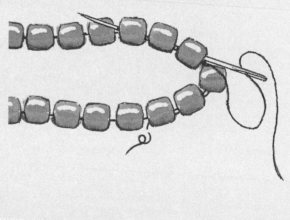

working with glues and adhesives

Adhesives play many roles in beaded jewelry. They can bond earring backings, help with thread security in bead weaving, or attach embellishments to beads. As we have seen on page 40, the four most commonly used adhesives in beaded jewelry making are two-part epoxy, instant or super glue, super tacky white glue, and clear nail polish or fray preventer.

strengthening knots

Instant glues, clear nail polish, or fray preventers can all be used to strengthen knots and prevent unraveling thread ends. Apply the product carefully to the knot or thread end, taking care to cover the area well without dripping or blobbing it onto the beads in the design.

attaching earring posts or pins

To attach an earring post or pin back to a bead or button, use two-part epoxy glue. Prepare the bonding surfaces by sanding lightly and then wipe clean. Allow any moisture to dry. Mix the epoxy following the manufacturer's instructions and apply generously to the metal-post back or pin back. The glue should cover the area generously without oozing to the sides of the backing. Firmly apply the post or pin to the bead and hold for about a minute to set the position. Allow a complete curing time of 24 hours.

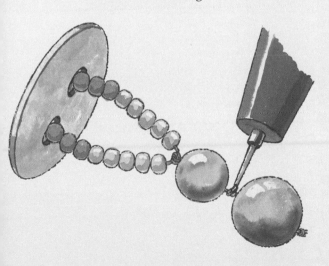

clasps

Some kind of closure is needed for most strung beads and will probably be the first thing you want to learn about. It's a good place to start because the length and style of the fastener will affect the length of the string of beads and needs to be considered at the design stage.

The most common fasteners for single-string necklaces and bracelets are the lobster-claw clasp, spring-ring clasp, hook-and-eye, S-clasp, toggle, barrel, pearl closure, and magnetic clasps (see page 31). Some of these come with a safety catch or chain built in, which is worth considering for expensive or heavy jewelry.

Before using it to make a piece of jewelry, always test the clasp by trying it on the intended part of your body to eliminate faulty or unmanageable ones. For a necklace, hold it behind your neck to see if it fastens easily. For a bracelet, check whether the clasp can be opened and closed easily with one hand.

All forms of clasps will come with a closed loop to attach to the string of beads. Be aware that you also need to consider a way of allowing movement in the clasp area to prevent strain. The closure is the most vulnerable part of any piece of jewelry and allowing movement at this juncture is crucial.

tip
Beware of barrel clasps, because they have a tendency to unscrew themselves unless they are attached to a very rigid cord. Closures with simple mechanics, like the S-clasp or toggle, are less likely to fail. The entire necklace has to be restrung if the closure fails, so it's worth spending money and time choosing a good one.

attaching a clasp using a split ring or jump ring

Perhaps the simplest method of attaching a clasp to the necklace or bracelet is to use a split ring or a jump ring. This will give the strings lots of room to move, improve the strength, and make it much easier to fasten. The split ring or jump ring is used between a closure loop on the clasp and a fixed ring attached to the strung ends of the necklace. It brings the two sides together because it can be opened and closed, whereas the rings on either side are soldered shut. Never attach the cord or thread of the necklace or bracelet directly to an unsoldered jump ring because the thread could slip through the opening crack. See pages 71 and 77 for more information about making, using, and closing jump rings.

Here a jump ring is used to attach the fixed ring of a toggle closure to the fixed ring, which is tied onto the strings of beads below. The tops of the bead strings are covered with a silver cone where they meet the fixed jump ring for a more professional finish.

attaching a clasp using crimp beads

Crimp beads (see page 29) are small tubular or round beads that are used to secure two parts of flexible beading wire (or other stringing material that cannot be knotted) together.

If you are using a strong material such as a beading wire to make a necklace or bracelet, the wire can loop directly onto the clasp and be secured with a crimp bead. It does not need a jump ring. However, make sure the loop attaching it to the closure is not too tight. The loop needs to pivot easily in all directions.

Crimp beads are closed by flattening them with pliers around the beading wire. This can be done with a pair of chain-nose pliers or crimping pliers (see pages 17–18).

Crimping pliers will give the crimp bead a smooth curled shape and are highly recommended. Crimping pliers have two holes in the nose. The first is oval shaped, used for closing the crimp, and the second is oval with a dip on one side.

1 To secure the crimp bead, slip it onto the beading wire. Loop the wire back through the crimp bead, including any jump rings or closures in the loop.

2 Position the crimp bead (with the wires in it) in the second oval of the pliers (the one with the dip), and close the pliers around the bead. You'll see it curl.

3 Position the same bead in the first oval, rotate it 90°, and close the pliers around the bead again so that you fold over the curled bead. Once your crimp bead is secure, trim off the excess wire. Now you have a good loop to hold your clasp. Add a crimp bead cover for a more professional finish if you like (see page 29).

attaching
cord closures

When attaching strung beads to a clasp, make a large loop on the beading wire so that it has plenty of room to pivot.

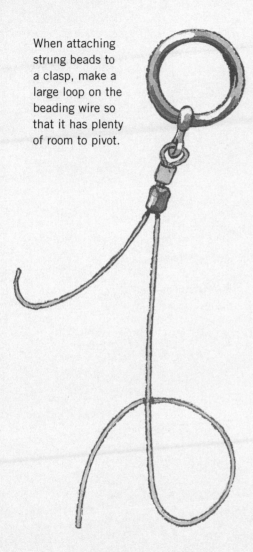

Cords can be attached to a clasp with a specially designed end coil or crimp end. Special crimp clasps are also available (see page 29). All of these are designed to fit around the end of the cord, giving it a tidy look. End coils and crimp ends have a loop for attaching to a clasp. Cord ends come in different sizes so be sure to buy one that is suitable for your chosen cord.

Close the end coil around the cord by applying pressure with a pair of pliers. You can also use glue to hold soft or slippery cords in place before crimping. After the glue is dry, test the security of the closure by pulling on the cord.

bead tips

Bead tips are also referred to as clamshells, knot cups, or calottes. They are used with soft stringing materials, such as threads or silk, to hide the knots. The thread ends are brought up through the hole at the bottom of the cup, knotted, glued (if necessary), trimmed, and then the sides of the cup are closed over the knot. The metal tongue is then made into a loop with pliers, which is attached to the clasp.

1 The thread is passed through the central hole in the bead tip to begin beading, in this case, a pair of earrings.

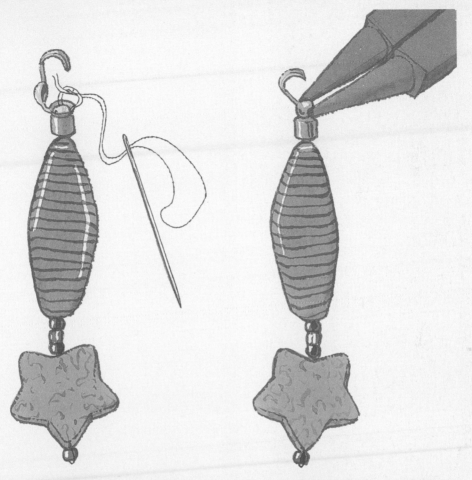

2 When the beading is complete, the thread is brought back up through the hole in the bead tip and knotted with the other end of the thread. This knot should be glued with clear nail polish or a fray preventer before the ends are trimmed.

3 Once the ends of the knot are trimmed, the cup of the bead tip is closed with a pair of pliers to hide the knot. The metal tongue of the bead tip is now ready to be shaped into a loop.

multiple strands

Pieces of jewelry that consist of a number of different strands of beads need special treatment to help the strands lie in a pleasing manner, rather than bunched up around the neckline.

spacer bars

Spacer or separator bars are used to keep strands of beads at an equal distance from one another, rather than forming a bunch. They are particularly useful in necklaces, where the curve of the neckline will otherwise force the strands of beads on top of one another.

You do not have to use all the holes in a spacer or separator bar. For example, in a 15-hole spacer bar that is about $1^3/4$ in (4 cm) long, you might only use three holes in the spacer bar if you are using $5/16$ in (8 mm) beads. The larger size of the beads would hide the unused holes in the spacer bar.

tip

Cones can help to reduce the bulk of beads along the back of the neckline by allowing a single strand at the back and multiple strands at the front.

end caps

An elegant method for bringing multiple strands together into a single closure is by using an end cone, also known as a dome or end cap. These can either be placed at the very back, next to the closure, or used along the front as a decorative element in a necklace design.

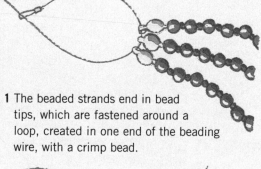

1 The beaded strands end in bead tips, which are fastened around a loop, created in one end of the beading wire, with a crimp bead.

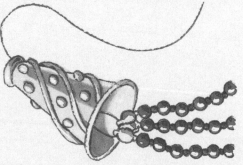

2 The beading wire is then brought up through the bead cone, which hides the joins of the three separate strands.

attaching a clasp

We have already seen how to attach a single strand of beads to a clasp or closure (see pages 50–51). However, if you want to include multiple strands of beads in a necklace or bracelet, there are different methods to consider.

The simplest way is to close each strand around one common, large jump ring. In this six-strand necklace, two strands of beads are held in each of three bead tips, which are attached to one common split ring. The split ring can then be attached to the closure of your choice. Here it is a toggle closure.

The three-strand connector, or reducer, is designed to make the closure of multiple strands more elegant. It has the advantage of spreading the strands flat at the closure point so that they lie better on the neckline. The three-strand connector can also be used as a chandelier for earring beads.

Beading wire is attached to this three-strand end by knotting the stringing material, which can then be pulled through to fit inside a bead with a larger hole. Be sure to leave a little slack in the thread so that the bead string can pivot on the closure. Alternatively beading wire can be attached with crimp beads.

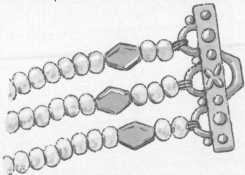

Some closures come with multiple loops. These obviously lend themselves to multistrand necklaces and bracelets and, like three-strand connectors, spread the strands so they lie flat.

making your own beads

There are many ways to make beads. However, some of the most common methods are impractical for a home craftsperson, and others are too specialized for the scope of this book. For instance, seed beads are made in factories in large batches, while techniques such as hot metalwork, lampworked or fused glass, and stone and gem carving require great craftsmanship and special tools to master. There are, however, several techniques you can use at home, with minimal equipment, to embellish or make your own beads. These also have the advantage of allowing you to design all aspects of the bead, from shape to size.

decorating wooden beads

Wooden beads are readily available in plain, painted, or stained designs and in many shapes and sizes. They are inexpensive and lightweight and can be further decorated at home with a matte or gloss surface. Their shape can even be changed by adding extensions in an air-drying clay that adheres well to the surface of the bead. Creative Paperclay, an air-drying clay available through doll-making suppliers, is excellent for this. This creates a different finish to polymer clay and makes an ideal surface for decorating with paint.

sculpting clay onto wooden beads

Prepare a work space with a bowl of water, an old cloth for cleaning your hands and tools, and a piece of white paper as a work surface. You may also like to have handy some sculpting tools or a manicurist's orange stick to help with tricky areas.

1 Wet the bead and begin by pressing clay onto the surface. Smooth away any cracks. Be careful to keep your bead holes clear of clay. Alternatively, you could use a kinked wire to hold the bead and keep track of your holes (see opposite).

2 When you have sculpted the clay to the desired shape, apply a drop of water to help smooth the final surface with your fingers. Let dry.

3 When the surface is no longer cold to the touch and it has become bone white in color, it is dry. This can take up to four days, depending on the temperature and thickness of clay. You may then carve or sand the surface if you wish.

4 Follow the instructions for painting wooden beads.

painting wooden beads

1 Begin by lightly sanding the surface of the bead to remove any glossy finish, which will prevent the new paint from adhering. Prepare beads for painting by running an 18-gauge copper wire through the hole. Kink or twist the wire on either side of the bead to hold it in place. This will keep the bead from rolling while you paint it. When you have finished painting, you can poke the wire into a foil tray while it dries.

2 Start by priming the surface of the bead with white or colored gesso. Allow to dry, then use an acrylic or oil-based paint to make the design. Build up layers of paint one at a time, allowing each to dry before continuing. A hair dryer will speed this process for the impatient bead maker.

3 When the painting is complete, you can embellish the surface with rhinestones or other flat decorations, sticking them in place with an epoxy glue. Then apply a coat of matte or gloss varnish, if you like, and let dry. Alternatively, touch up some parts of the bead with a gloss varnish and leave other areas matte to enhance the design.

tip
Acrylic paints can be used with many different media to change the surface of the bead. This could include adding glitter or a pumice texture. To add shimmer to your beads, use interference paints, which react with underlying layers of color, or metallic paints. There are also acrylic gouaches available, which give excellent matte results and show no brush marks.

polymer-clay beads

Polymer clay is a relatively new and versatile material for making beads. The clay hardens by baking in a regular oven without changing color or size. Once cured, the color will neither chip nor fade as a painted bead might.

Polymer clays are available under many brand names but they all work in essentially the same way. Some are softer for working with than others: remember, they can be mixed together to achieve the consistency you prefer.

The advantages of polymer clay beads are that they won't start to dry in the open air and you don't have to wait days for them to be ready. However, large beads made from polymer clay can be heavy; consider using a wooden bead and adding a layer of polymer clay on top (see page 56) if weight is an issue.

There are many colors and finishes available. Colors can be custom-blended from a mixture of those you can buy. Additives—such as bits of thread, glitter, seed beads, or sand—can be included in the clay to change its texture and appearance. Polymer clays can be painted, but they need to be fully prepared by sanding and priming first.

polymer-clay beads

conditioning the clay

All polymer clays need to be conditioned thoroughly before use. As well as making the clay much easier to work, conditioning mixes the components to make a stronger, more durable finished piece.

To condition by hand, start by warming and rolling a small piece of clay in your hands. Roll it into a long sausage, fold it back onto itself, and then roll it out again. Repeat until the polymer stretches (instead of breaking) when you pull it apart.

If you use polymer clay frequently, consider buying a food processor and pasta machine to speed up its preparation. (Never share these machines with food preparation.) Dice the polymer into 3/8 in (1 cm) cubes and put them in the food processor. Process until the clay forms a lump. Run the lump through the pasta machine on the thickest setting. Fold in half and run it through again. Repeat 10 to 15 times until the clay is soft and workable, stretching without crumbling.

making a hole

It is easier to shape the beads first, then create a hole before baking. Special needle tools are available for this, or make your own by setting a long needle into a polymer clay handle and baking. Minimize distortion by rotating the piercing tool as you gently push it through the bead. Stop pushing when you see the tip come out the other side, then pierce again from the exit-hole side.

Some people prefer to drill holes in the clay after baking to prevent distortion to the shape or pattern. This is best carried out with a small hand drill and pin vice. Try hand drilling on a few test beads before working with designs you have spent a lot of time on.

baking

Most brands bake at 275°F (135°C), but check the manufacturer's instructions. If the temperature is too low, the polymer will not completely fuse and the finished piece may be easily broken. If the temperature is too high, the polymer may burn and release noxious fumes. Consider baking your beads for a little extra time than that recommended to make sure they are fully cured. This will not harm them.

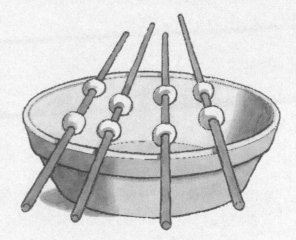

Suspend the beads on bamboo skewers over a baking bowl while they bake, to prevent them becoming misshapen. Alternatively, rest them on a nest of soft polyester fiberfill. The beads may pick up a small amount of its texture, but this can be sanded off after the beads are baked.

finishing the beads

Once the beads have cooled, they can be sanded, buffed, and/or carved. To sand the beads, use wet-and-dry sandpaper and dip the bead and paper in water from time to time as you work. Begin with 320-grade paper and continue up in stages, finishing with 1000-grade for a refined finish. After sanding, buff with a soft cloth. For a glossy finish, apply a polymer-clay varnish. If you wish to embellish the beads with flat rhinestones, use Super Glue to stick them securely in place.

fabric beads

Beads can easily be created out of fabrics. The materials are inexpensive and often at hand. Fabrics can be gathered at the hole edges around existing beads or sewn into shapes and stuffed.

fabric, felt, and crochet bead choker

stuffed fabric shapes

You will need fabric scraps, polyester fiberfill, scissors, sewing thread, needles, pins, and invisible nylon thread. A sewing machine will speed up the process but is not essential. Use the following instructions to make a disc-shaped bead.

1 Draw a circle onto a piece of cardboard and cut out to make a template. Cut two discs from a piece of fabric, allowing a 3/16 in (5 mm) seam allowance. Apply a fray preventer to the edges of the fabric, if necessary, and allow to dry.

2 With right sides together, stitch the two fabric discs together, leaving a small gap in the seam. If you are using a machine, choose a very small stitch length. Turn the fabric disc right sides out and stuff with a little polyester fiberfill. Sew the opening shut using an invisible stitch with nylon thread.

3 Decorate the bead with embroidery, stitched beads, or rhinestones if you like. Then use an awl to poke a hole through the bead from one side to the other, carefully placing the tool between the stitches of the seams. A long darning needle can then be used to thread a cord or ribbon through the bead. Make a knot in the cord or ribbon on either side of the bead to hold it in position.

beading a bead

Larger beads can be created using small beads in many different ways. The most common method is to weave small beads around a larger base bead. Remember when choosing your core bead that the final size will be larger once you have woven the covering. To make a pendant for a necklace, use a glass bead at the core to give it some weight. For earrings, a light wooden or plastic core bead is suitable. You can use seed beads of all sizes and shapes to cover a bead. On larger beads, small beads in glass, stone, or metal can also be used.

Various bead-weaving stitches can be used to cover a bead, including peyote, netting, and right angle. Right-angle weaving is perhaps the best because the seed beads face in many directions, making a surface that is very forgiving and attractive. However, the simplest way to cover a bead with smaller beads is to simply wrap it with strings of seed beads. Choose a core bead that coordinates well with your seed beads because it will be visible in the finished work. It should also have a fairly large hole because the beading thread will need to pass through it repeatedly.

These embellished beads show a random placement of different-colored beads in the weaving (left) and loops of seed beads around the top and middle (right).

simple strung bead wrapping

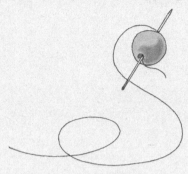

1 Thread a beading needle with a long piece of doubled beading thread and bring the needle down through the hole of the base bead. Secure a 4 in (10 cm) thread tail with your thumb as you work.

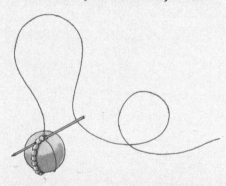

2 String the correct number of seed beads to cover half the circumference of the core bead and then bring the thread down through the core-bead hole and out the bottom (working in the same direction through the hole as you did initially). The seed beads should cover the surface from one hole to the other. You may wish to knot the tail of the thread with the working thread at this point to secure the end.

3 String the same number of seed beads again and repeat until the whole core bead is covered at the ends. There will be gaps between the bead strings in the middle where the core bead shows through because the circumference of the bead is larger in the middle.

right-angle weave beaded bead

These instructions are for a $3/8$ in (1 cm) core bead but will work for a large variety of sizes without much alteration.

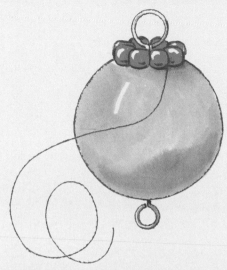

1 To begin the bead, make a loop of seed beads: thread eight beads, leaving a $2^3/8$ in (6 cm) tail. Tie a knot so the beads form a circle and bring your needle through the first two or three beads.

2 Begin by making a "handle" for the core bead from 18-gauge copper wire. This will hold the seed beads on to begin with and help your grip. You will discard the wire when the bead is finished. Using pliers, bend a loop into one end of the wire. Place the woven circle of beads on the wire through the center, and then place the core bead on. With your pliers, make another loop and cut the wire. The wire should fit snugly so that the work does not move around.

tips

It may be helpful to weave a band of straightforward right-angle weave before you begin, to familiarize yourself with the pattern of the weave. A band of four rows in an 11° bead or small glass bead can make a simple bracelet with which you can learn the stitch and produce a finished piece of jewelry.

If there are gaps in the beading due to uneven increasing and decreasing, these can easily be hidden by weaving beads into them or embellishing when the bead is complete.

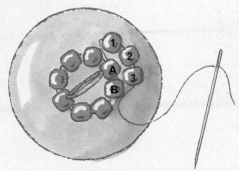

3 Work a right-angle weave (see page 118) over the surface of the core bead. Thread on three beads, then take the needle back through beads A, 1, 2, and 3 and then through bead B.

4 Thread on three beads again. If you were not increasing you would just add two beads. However, as the circumference of the core bead widens, you need to increase. Go back through bead 3, bead B, and come out through bead 4.

5 Add two beads (you are only increasing at every other bead) then go through bead C and back through beads 4, 7 and 8, and come out through bead D.

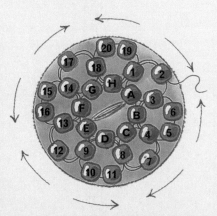

6 Continue weaving beads, alternating adding three (an increase) and two beads with every other group. To complete the circle, pass the needle through beads H and 1, add two beads (19 and 20) and come back through beads 18 and H. Bring the needle up through beads 1 and 2 to begin the next round.

7 Continue beading, adding increases when the beads are becoming too snug around the core bead. This is not very precise because it depends on the size and shape of your seed beads and core bead. When you have gone past the middle of the core bead, you will need to decrease.

8 To decrease, skip over a bead in the outer circle. Toward the end of the core bead, you will need to decrease drastically so that you end with your needle going through eight beads. Weave in the ends and remove your bead from the wire.

felt beads

Felt beads look great, plain or embellished, on a handmade felt cord. They also look fantastic strung next to beads of other materials.

Making felt beads is simple and inexpensive. You need very few materials to begin with. Washed, carded, and dyed wool roving can be bought from weaving, spinning, and felt-making suppliers in a large variety of colors. You will need very little to make a bead so buy the smallest quantity possible of a fine merino wool roving. Sometimes yarn suppliers sell mixed bags of colors in small quantities. These are a good value for the felt bead maker.

wool top

making a round felt bead

Expect to make about three beads before you begin to feel comfortable with the process and know how much water and soap to use. Begin with a medium-size bead and try other sizes once you are familiar with the process. Larger beads take longer to felt, while it can be more difficult to achieve an even finish on smaller beads. Begin by gathering together the following materials: a towel to cover your work surface and a spare one nearby; a bowl of ice-cold water and a bowl of freshly boiled water (keep the hot water over a fondue-pot warmer or stove); a squeeze or sprinkle bottle with a solution of hot water and 10% baby shampoo (when not in use this soap solution may be left to stand in the bowl of boiled water to keep warm); a slotted spoon to lift the beads from the hot water; a bar of olive oil or other gentle soap resting on a plate nearby; scissors and a ruler.

tips

An awl can be used to poke a hole through the bead, while a large-eyed darning needle coaxed with a pair of pliers can be used to thread different kinds of cord through the bead.

Other materials may be included in the felting process, such as wool yarns, silk fibers and fabrics, and a variety of threads.

1 Cut a length of wool roving about 2³/4 in (7 cm) long. Divide it into four equal sections. Spread out and tease the first three of these so that they each form a pile of fibers that is roughly square. Divide the final section into two groups, one that is about an eighth of the other, and spread these into two square piles of fiber. The thin pile will be your bead "skin" and should be placed to one side for now.

2 Take one of the four piles and lay it on top of another pile with the fibers at a right angle. Repeat this with the next layer, laying it with the fibers in the same direction as the first, but at a right angle to the second. Place the fourth layer with the fibers at a right angle to the last pile. You now have four layers of spread-out wool roving lying on top of each other, with each successive layer lying at a right angle to the one before.

3 Sprinkle hot soapy water onto the stacked piles so they are wet but not drenched. Dip the soap into hot water and lightly lather your hands. Place your hand down on the pile of tops and pull it up. Begin gently rolling the tops in your hand to form an airy ball. Don't apply pressure. The tops should be wet enough to hold together but not so wet they are hard to manipulate. Continue rolling, applying very light pressure. Examine the bead: if it is developing large cracks, you may need more water and soap.

4 Roll the soapy bead in the final "skin" layer and then roll it in your soapy hands. You may use a different color or mix in other fibers at this point.

5 If the bead looks good, with no cracks, start to roll with more pressure. If there are still cracks, use a bit more fiber to smooth over rough areas. Roll the bead for a few more minutes. It should not be too wet or it will be difficult to control. Squeeze the bead to see how much more it can condense. Beads can be left slightly spongy or rolled until very hard. This is a personal preference.

6 When you are happy with the denseness of the bead, pop it into the boiled water and squeeze out the soap with the slotted spoon. Lift the bead from the hot water into the cold water. The change in temperatures will shock the fibers, completing the felting procedure. Remove the bead and squeeze out excess water. Let it dry.

WORKING WITH WIRE

Many pieces of jewelry can be made with wire, beads, and a few simple tools. You can form jump rings, chains, earring hooks, closures, and necklace links without ever going near a soldering iron. Try practicing the techniques in this chapter with 18-gauge copper wire. It is an inexpensive and easy wire to manipulate. Have on hand some other gauges to test designs as well, such as 20, 21, and 22 gauge. Once you become familiar with the techniques and tools, you might like to make these components in silver or other wires.

cutting wire

Wires used in jewelry must always be cut flush and filed so that there are no sharp ends, burrs, or snags. It is best to get in the habit of keeping the ends of your uncut wire flush-cut and filed.

1 It is important when making pairs of wire components, such as kidney-shaped earring wires, that you measure and mark two identical pieces of wire before you begin. Use a clear plastic ruler to measure and mark with a permanent pen in a circle around the wire. The pen marks can be removed with steel wool when the jewelry is finished.

tip

Steel wool and polishing cloths are used to polish silver, copper, and brass wires. If the silver wire has been dipped in liver of sulfur to oxidize and antique it, polishing it with steel wool (grade 0000) will remove any excess chemicals and darkener. Finish by buffing the piece with a polishing cloth.

2 Flush cutters (see page 16) are specifically designed to create a flush end. The flat side of the flush cutter makes a smooth end on the wire. The beveled side will leave the cut wire with a sharp end. Try cutting a piece of wire to examine the two cuts; use a magnifying glass if necessary. Finished jewelry pieces should always have wire cut with the flush end. When cutting wire, always restrain the cut end with your fingers to prevent it from flying away.

3 Completed wirework can have snags and points, even when it has been cut flush. File wire ends with needle files (see page 19) by running the ends of the wire back and forth across the file.

shaping wire

Wire can be shaped using fingers, pliers, a wire jig (see page 74), or a combination of these tools. You will find that a good pair of pliers are particularly versatile and portable.

bending wire with pliers

A few different pairs of pliers will make a limitless variety of bends. Pliers come in different shapes and circumferences to help aid the bending process. Round-nose pliers are often chosen for bending wire when making a loop shape with the wire, such as an eyepin. Pliers with a flat side are used to give the wire a sharp angle or flatten it.

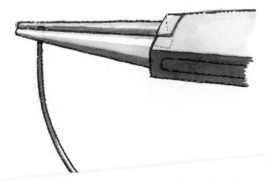

1 Place the wire in the mouth of the pliers, keeping the end flush with the top edge of the pliers. You should be able to see the end but not feel it poking out.

2 Twist your wrist, holding the pliers away from you, and use the thumb of your other hand to press the wire against the barrel of the pliers. As the wire bends around the pliers, you will need to open and rotate them to complete a full loop.

adjusting loops

To open and close loops, such as those on jump rings and eyepins, use one or two pairs of pliers, depending on the thickness of the wire. With each pair, grab an end of the loop where they join. Move one end up and the other down to make a gap without opening the circle outward. Close the loop by grabbing the two ends with the pliers and gently grind them back and forth until you hear them rubbing together. This will indicate a good fit.

making an eye or loop opening

You will need to make an eye in the end of a headpin or an eyepin to attach it to other components in a piece of jewelry. There are many other uses for eyes as well. For instance, a length of wire can be bent with an eye on either side of a bead to make a unit of a chain.

1 Place the wire between the jaws of your round-nose pliers. The position of the wire—farther up or down the jaws—will determine the size of the eye. Make sure the end of the wire is flush with the top edge of the pliers so it does not stick out. See Bending Wire with Pliers, step 1, on page 71.

3 Hold the P-shaped wire vertically, with the loop facing away from you. Grasp the straight part of the wire just above where the loop joins it, with the tip of your chain-nose pliers. Rotate your wrist toward you, while at the same time using the index finger of your other hand to press down on the neck of the eyepin near the joint. This is a very slight movement to bring the loop into line above the rest of the wire.

2 Rotate the pliers away from your body and press down on the wire with the thumb of your other hand. When you can go no farther, release the wire, reposition your pliers, and close the gap. You will now have a P-shaped loop.

4 To perfect the shape, place the lower jaw of the round-nose pliers inside the eye, making sure the wire wraps snugly around the pliers. With your thumb pressing against the neck, rotate the pliers until the eye sits directly above the neck of the pin. Straighten the neck with flat-nose pliers if necessary.

twisting and coiling wire

Two wires can be twisted around one another to make a single twisted braid. This can then be used as if it were a single wire to make jump rings or other wire components.

twisting wire

Dead-soft wire is the best choice for twisting. There are special tools available to make this process faster and easier, but it can be done with a standard electric drill.

Start by working with 6–9 ft (2–3 m) of wire. Fold the length of wire in half and insert the two ends in a grip fixed to an electric drill. Hook the other, looped, end over a hook fixed into the wall. Turn the drill on: the wires will twist around one another. When they are tightly twisted, the end on the hook will usually snap. Cut and file the wire ends as usual.

coiling wire

A piece of wire can be coiled around a central wire core. This looks very different from the twisted wires previously described. In fact, you can even coil twisted wires around a core for a really interesting design.

1 Cut a length of wire for the core and smooth the ends with a file. Alternatively, use a piece of wire with an eye loop bent into either end. By wrapping this with twisted wire you can create an attractive jewelry component.

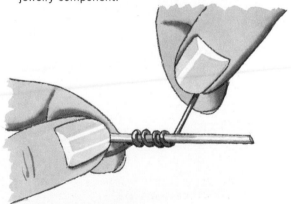

2 Hold the core wire in one hand and coil uncut wire around the core with your other hand. When you have finished coiling, cut the ends of the coiled wire flush and file smooth.

wire jigs

Wire jigs (see page 19) are designed for bending wires. There are a number of commercial models available, but it is easy enough to make your own. This will allow you to test its usefulness before investing in one.

making a wire jig

You will need a piece of wood about 6 x 3 1/4 in (15 x 8 cm) and about 1 3/4 in (4 cm) thick. The following design is good for making eyepins with three loops, which can be used to hang multiple dangles on an earring, for example.

1 Insert a screw into the center of the block of wood. This will be used to anchor the wire as you work.

2 Hammer three nails into the wood above the screw. The first nail should be 1 3/4 in (4 cm) away from the screw, directly above it. The second and third nails should be 1 in (2.5 cm) above the screw and 3/8 in (1 cm) to each side. There will be a 3/4 in (2 cm) distance between the two bottom nails.

3 Use a hack saw to cut off the nail heads. File the tops down a little until the nails are smooth and won't cut your fingers as you use the jig.

using the jig

The jig can be used to make a variety of bent wire shapes by wrapping the wire around all or some of the nails. For instance, a figure-eight eye closure can be made using just the lower two nails.

A three-loop clover eyepin can be made with 21-gauge wire by following the wrapping directions in the illustration above. Cut both ends of the wire flush, being sure to leave enough straight length for a bead and/or an eye loop. File smooth.

hammering wire

Traditional metalworking techniques include heating and hammering items into a desired shape. For the cold wireworker, hammering is still a useful technique to create shapes or harden and strengthen metal.

flattening wire

A hammer can be used to create a flat, teardrop-shaped end on an eyepin. You will need a metal hammer head to flatten and change the shape and surface of the metal. The shape of the hammer head will also affect the shape of the wire: if the edge of the hammer is constructed with an abrupt angle, an angle or dent will appear in the piece being pounded.

hardening wire

Hammering with a plastic mallet will harden and strengthen wire without changing its shape. If your wire is in a coil, use a plastic mallet to hammer it into straight lengths before you begin working. You can also use a plastic mallet to straighten out lengths that you have mistakenly bent. Be aware though, that the more it is hammered, the harder the wire gets, making it more difficult to work. Avoid hammering two pieces of wire that cross each other as it will fatigue the metal, possibly causing it to break.

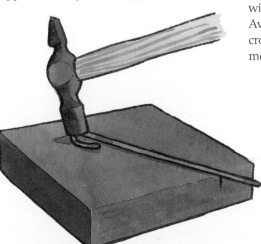

Place one end of the wire on an anvil or bench block. Hammer until the end is flat, decreasing the strength of the hammering as you go up the wire. Test to make sure the end is large enough to keep the bead on the eyepin. File off any sharp edges or snags.

making fastenings and findings

This section gives examples of some of the most common wire components that can be made with pliers and cutters. These can also be shaped on a homemade or commercial wire jig. A 21-gauge, half-hard, round silver wire has been used for these examples. Gauges 18, 20, and 22 may also be suitable, but try them out first.

headpins

Store-bought headpins are usually made by melting a bead of silver to create a ball end. However, it is possible to make headpins by hammering the end to create a flat teardrop shape (see page 75). Another method of creating a headpin is to coil the end.

1 Cut a piece of wire about 2³/4 in (7 cm) long with flush ends. Use a longer piece of wire if you are going to place a large bead on it. File the ends smooth. Use round-nose pliers at a thin point to make a small loop at one end.

2 To continue making the coil, hold the small loop flat between the jaws of a pair of nylon-nose pliers (or wrap tape around a pair of flat-nose pliers). Use your thumb to bend the straight part of the wire around the first coil.

3 Make the coil as small or as large as you like, but remember to leave enough room to allow for beads and a loop at the top for connecting it.

eyepins

Eyepins can be bought in several lengths and gauges, but you may want to make your own. It can be difficult to find the correct gauge eyepins for pearls, for example.

Follow the instructions for making an eye loop on page 72, using a 2³/4 in (7 cm) length of wire. You can create a variation of this design by hammering the upper area of the eye with a metal hammer. This will flatten the metal around the eye to create a decorative effect. After hammering, you will need to coax the circle closed with your round-nose pliers.

jump rings

Jump rings are simple wire circles with a multitude of uses. They join one component to the next, allowing movement between them.

The size of the finished jump rings will depend on the diameter of the mandrel (see page 20) or pliers used in their making. Use a 6 in (15 cm) length of wire to make multiple jump rings of the same size. It is difficult to use smaller lengths of wire when wrapping because there is little to grab hold of, and longer lengths can be unwieldy. Wrapping around pliers may be a little trickier to master than wrapping around a mandrel, but pliers do have the advantage of giving you many possible diameters with just one tool.

2 If you are using round-nose pliers, use a permanent pen to mark the place on the pliers where the circumference matches the size of ring you want to create. Then wrap the wire around the mark for one full loop. Move the wire up the pliers so that the next loop will be in the same place and wrap again. Continue so that each loop is the same circumference.

1 Use your fingers to wrap the wire around the mandrel, keeping the wire flush against it and creating a number of tight rings next to one another.

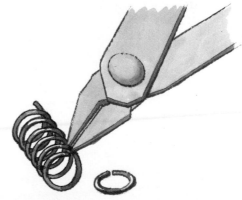

3 Slide the wire coil off the mandrel or pliers. Use flush cutters to cut the first coil end in line with the beginning of the wire. You will then need to trim the coil with the other side of the flush cutters before cutting the next jump ring, so that it starts with a flush end. Use a jeweler's file to smooth the ends of the wire and remove any burrs.

making clasps

Elegant necklace clasps can be created at home using the eye closure and one of the two hooks shown here. There are many different ways to make clasps and closures but these two solutions require only pliers, cutters, a file, and wire. Choose 20-gauge wire, ideally half-hard.

To add the clasp to a beaded item, just hook a bead tip onto the looped part of either hook or eye. To add it to a wire project or necklace finished with a crimp bead, open the loop a little and hook it over the end of the wire piece, then close the loop again using flat-nose pliers. The appropriate length of wire for each component will depend on the circumference of your pliers and the gauge of your wire. It is a good idea to make an example in a cheap copper wire to test the results before trying it in a more expensive wire like silver. Once you have found the right length, make a note of it, including which gauge of wire was used and where on the pliers the wire was bent.

figure-eight eye closure

1 Cut a 4.25 cm (1¹³⁄₁₆ in) piece of wire with flush ends. File the ends to make them smooth. Place the wire in the mouth of the round-nose pliers at their thickest point, keeping the end flush with the top edge of the pliers. You should be able to see the end but not feel it poking out.

2 Twist your wrist, holding the pliers away from you, and use the thumb of your other hand to press the wire against the barrel of the pliers. As the wire bends around the pliers you will need to open and rotate them to complete a full loop.

3 Repeat the same procedure on the other end of the wire, but this time the loop should be facing in the other direction to make a figure-eight. You have chosen the right length of wire if the two ends of the wire meet. If they do not, either cut a different length of wire or create the loops on another part of the pliers.

hook one

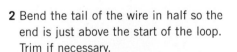

1 Cut a 2³/4 in (7 cm) piece of wire with flush ends. File the ends to make them smooth. Using round-nose pliers, bend ¹/2 in (1.25 cm) of the wire away from you at a 90° angle. Then curl the wire toward you, around the pliers, to create a loop. Alternatively, follow the directions for making an eye loop (see page 72).

2 Bend the tail of the wire in half so the end is just above the start of the loop. Trim if necessary.

3 Use flat-nose pliers to squeeze the two sides of the long loop together flush up against each other. Use round-nose pliers to bend the doubled wire in half by pushing the wire around the pliers to form a graceful curve.

hook two

1 Follow steps 1 and 2 of making the figure-eight eye closure (opposite), this time using a length of wire 2¹/2 in (6.5 cm) long and the tip of the pliers to create a smaller loop. Use flat-nose pliers to flatten the tip of the curl.

2 Use round-nose pliers, at their largest point, to make a large loop on the opposite end of the wire. Hold the wire with the small loop at the top facing toward you, and the larger loop at the bottom. Twist your wrist away from you.

3 Use round-nose pliers at their thickest point to bend the wire into a hook, placing them a little higher than halfway up the wire. Bend the wire in the opposite direction of the previous loop.

french ear wires

These ear wires are also referred to as fishhooks. A headpin or eyepin with beads can be attached to the hook to make a simple pair of earrings.

1 Follow steps 1 and 2 of making the figure-eight eye closure (see page 78), this time using two lengths of wire 2 in (5 cm) long and the thin end of the pliers to create a small loop on each length of wire. Make sure the two loops are identical.

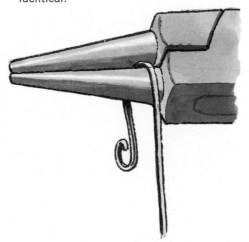
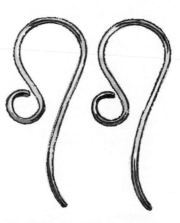

2 With the thickest part of the round-nose pliers, grasp the straight part of one wire approximately 1/4 in (6 mm) below the loop, with the loop facing up and toward you. Use your thumb to bend the wire around the pliers so that it almost touches the other side, leaving a 1/8 in (3 mm) gap. Repeat for the other wire, using the same point on the pliers so the loops match.

3 The next step is a very small, subtle movement. Hold the straight end of the wire uppermost with the loop facing away from you. Use the middle of the pliers to bend the wire slightly toward you, about 1/4 in (6 mm) from the top.

using ready-made chain

Most beading shops sell a variety of chains on a spool. This chain can be cut into lengths suitable for necklaces, bracelets, or earrings. To complete a necklace or bracelet, you need to attach the chain to a closure with split jump rings. Beaded charms made with headpins and eyepins can be used to embellish the design.

Simple earrings can be made by linking one or more chains to an ear-wire loop. Again, charms can be linked to the chain with wire, headpins, or eyepins.

other wire techniques

Wire can be used in many different ways. It will make a stiffer structure than cords or thread but this can be useful for creating shapes and holding objects. Use it in place of yarns for knitting with beads.

beading on fine wire

Fine wire can also be used as a beading cord for seed beads. The wire can then be knitted, crocheted, or bent into other shapes, such as flowers.

To knit or crochet with wire, follow the directions on pages 156–167 using a 26-gauge wire or finer. Both knitting and crocheting will create a very open mesh, which allows the beads to be seen easily. This mesh can be made into a variety of shapes that will hold their form in a way that other yarns will not.

wire wrapping

Wire wrapping is a method of jewelry design and creation that is done by hand. It involves the use of tools to bind and twist wires together around an object with no hole. Some of the basic techniques include twisting the wire, wrapping a wire bundle, crimping or flattening the wrap, and shaping. It is possible to incorporate any shape or finish, using any material from gemstones to pottery shards in the wrapping.

It is important to straighten wire before starting this technique and to keep wraps neat and straight on the front side as the project progresses. Wire ends should be

cut flush and tucked under wraps where possible. The specimens used in wire-wrapped jewelry could be rough, tumbled, faceted, carved, or cabochon-cut specimens. In addition to wrapping a gemstone, wire-wrapped designs can stand alone in rings, bracelets, brooches, and pendants.

beaded flowers

There is an old tradition of making flower shapes out of strung seed beads and wire. An infinite variety of shapes and forms can be created using fine-gauge wires and 11° beads. Minimal tools are needed, because the wire is so fine it can be cut with nail clippers and bent with just fingers.

The most suitable wires for creating beaded flowers are sold on spools in a variety of colors. Match the wire color to the predominant bead color to make it most invisible. You can change wire color within a design. The wire used for making the structural elements of flowers is usually 28-gauge, while 26-gauge may be used for larger petals and leaves. For lacing (the beaded fill that covers the structure of the flowers) and assembling, use 30- or 32-gauge wire. Flower stems should be made from either 16-, 18- or 20-gauge wires to add strength.

The best beads to use are 11° because they are large enough to allow the wire to pass through several times and still look very delicate. Larger beads can be used for accents in the center of flowers. String the beads onto the wire before the wire is bent into shape.

tip
Wrap the flower stems in floral tape to hide the joints and finish the look. Floral tape is available in a range of colors, including greens, browns, and white. It is very easy to use and sticks to itself as you pull it taut and wrap it around the wire.

a simple beaded flower

1 Cut 1 yd (approximately 1 m) of wire per flower. First, make the ring of outer petals. Make a small bend in the wire about 8 in (20 cm) from one end. Thread on 24 seed beads and move them along the wire until they reach the bend.

2 Bend the wire to form a loop for the first petal shape. Twist the wire at the bottom of the loop several times to secure the beads in place.

3 Repeat the process to make four more petals, twisting the wire around the center of the flower each time to secure the petals.

4 The inner petals are made in the same way as the outer ones, but with fewer beads and smaller loops. Thread on 16 seed beads for each petal. Make an inner petal inside each outer petal.

5 To finish the flower, thread a pearl bead onto the 8 in (20 cm) of wire that was kept free in step 1. Pull the wire over the center of the flower so that the pearl bead sits in this position, covering the mass of twisted wires at the center. Fold the wire to the back of the flower and twist it together with the other end of the wire.

6 Cut a length of 18- or 20-gauge wire for the stem. Wrap the flower wire ends around the stem wire to secure the flower in place. Apply hot glue or epoxy to hold the flower in the preferred position. When dry, wrap the stem and flower wires with floral tape if you like.

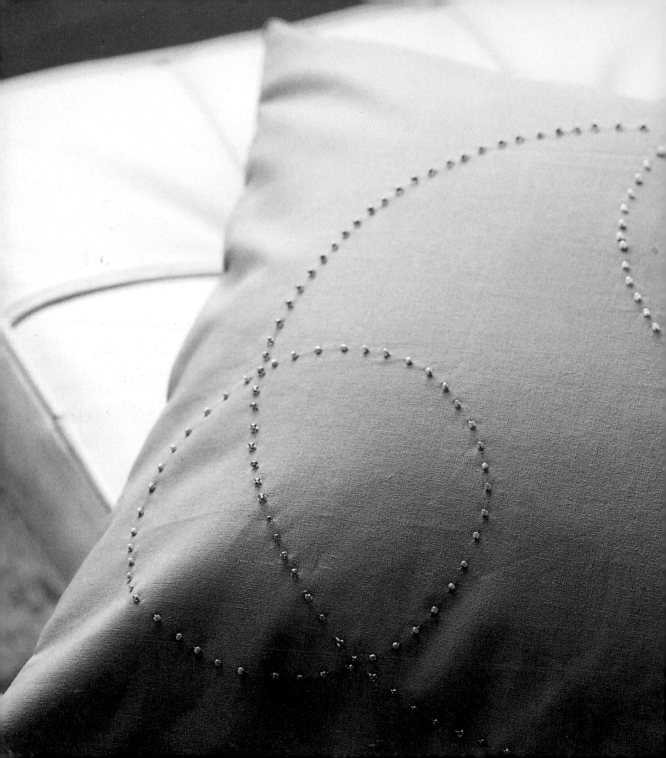

STITCHING AND WEAVING

There are many ways of using beads and stitches together. These include embroidery, weaving, knitting, and crocheting. Within each of these techniques there are many possible stitches that can create great variation in your designs. This chapter demonstrates each of the possibilities you can use with your beads.

knotting

Knots are used in beaded jewelry for both functional and decorative purposes. Macramé knots and Chinese knots are primarily decorative knots, although they often serve a practical purpose as well. The other knots described in this section are fundamental to any beadwork that uses beading threads and cords, because they are used to attach closures, begin and end work, and join threads.

weaver's knot

The weaver's knot is often used to secure two cord or thread ends together. When finishing a thread, leave a length of about 5 in (12.5 cm) with which to make the weaver's knot.

Loop the end back on itself and loop the end of the new thread. Work the ends of the new thread through the loop of the other thread as shown. Later, the thread ends can be woven back into the work.

overhand knot

This knot is used between beads in traditional pearl necklaces to keep the beads apart and protect the delicate pearls from rubbing against each other. It is used in other types of necklace too, because it provides a nice articulation and helps the necklace to drape well. It can be made with one or more strands.

Make a loop and pass the working end through it. Move the loose knot to the place you would like it to be and then pull the ends to tighten the knot.

slipknot

The slipknot is a very useful knot that can expand and contract. It is the basis for crochet stitches and is often used to begin beading projects. You can make a slipknot with the end of a thread or in the middle of a length.

1 Make a loop with the thread, creating an X where two pieces cross. Grab hold of the piece of thread that passes over the top of the lower one in the X, and bring a loop of this strand behind and through the loop that has been created.

2 Put this new loop through the old loop and pull down to create the slipknot. The short end of the yarn can be pulled to close the knot.

square knot

This knot is used in necklace strands, bead weaving, and other techniques to secure the threading material. It is a good, secure, all-purpose knot.

1 Beginning with two thread ends, overlap them, with thread A on top. Fold the A end underneath thread B and bring it back over the top of B.

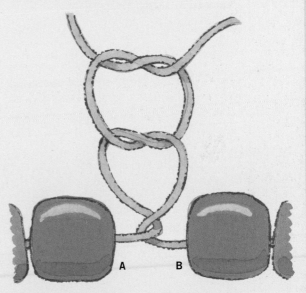

2 Lay thread A (which is now coming from the right-hand side) over thread B, in through the knot, and then bring it out toward you and pull the ends tight. This sequence will give you a secure knot.

simple sliding knot

This is a simple knot used to fasten two ends of a leather cord to make an adjustable-length necklace. A more decorative version can be made with Chinese button knots (see pages 92–93).

1 Overlap the two ends of the thong at the back of the necklace and tie an overhand knot in each of the thong ends, carrying the sides of the necklace through the center of each knot.

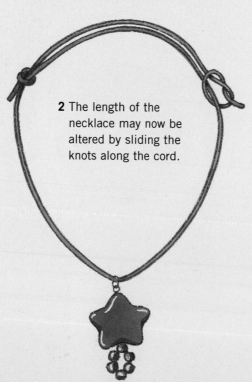

2 The length of the necklace may now be altered by sliding the knots along the cord.

macramé knots

Macramé knots are usually worked in a sturdy material like leather, satin cord, or waxed linen cord that allows the knots to have a distinct character. They can include beads or be used to make a cord end for necklaces. The rigidity of the material will make it easier to form the knots. Be careful to choose beads that have a big enough hole to accommodate the cord, such as lampworked glass or ceramic beads. The half hitch and double half hitch are the most commonly used knots in macramé beaded jewelry.

These knots are used in jewelry with macramé cording and they can be worked with different colors and more threads. Typically, four threads are secured to a cushion with a pin or attached to a board with nails in it.

tip

You can make a board to hold your macramé knots while you work. Simply hammer nails into a piece of wood and then loop the tops of the threads around them. An alternative method is to stick a pin through the top overhand knot of your work and then into a firm cushion.

half-hitch knot and double half-hitch knot

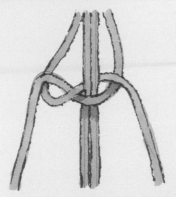

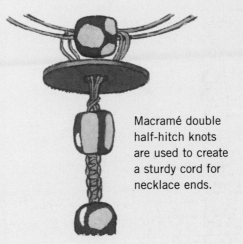

Macramé double half-hitch knots are used to create a sturdy cord for necklace ends.

1 Hold the two center threads taut while you alternate the outside threads, forming loops over and under them. Pull these tight, forming a boxy knot.

2 In the half-hitch knot (above left) the thread on the left will always go over (or under) the threads in the middle, creating a spiral, whereas the double half-hitch knot (above right) will have the left-hand thread alternating over and under the middle threads each time it is worked.

chinese knots

There is a large variety of decorative knots that are referred to as Chinese knots. These are usually made with silk or satin cords, which allow the knots to be moved into place on the cord. Again, the cords must be quite rigid to make the knotting possible. Be careful to choose beads that have a big enough hole to accommodate the cord.

These knots can be shaped in your hands or worked on a corkboard with pins to hold the loops in place before tightening into the final knot. The second method is easier. There are many different decorative knots. The most fundamental Chinese knot is the button knot. It can be worked at the end of a cord to make a decorative finish, or in the middle of the cord to space beads. It can also be made with two cords to create a sliding loop.

the button knot

Practice tying this knot with 1 yd (approximately 1 m) of satin cord. A smooth cord is needed to make it easier to manipulate the knot. Start about 4 in (10 cm) from the left-hand end of the cord, and concentrate on getting all the unders and overs correctly aligned and creating a neat, round knot. The position of the finished knot is not important at this stage, because it can be moved easily.

1 Make a loop in the cord. Hold the loop between your thumb and index finger of your non-knotting hand, or pin to a board. Make another loop over the top of the first loop.

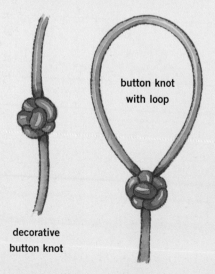

button knot
with loop

decorative
button knot

tip
Glue is usually painted onto the wrong side of the knot to secure and stiffen it. A solution of white glue or nail polish is also painted on cord ends to prevent them from unraveling. In the case of flat decorative knots, a few stitches with a fine sewing or beading thread on the back will secure it.

2 Take the end down through the loop on the right, up through the middle, and down through the left loop. Notice the central area that has been formed. This will be important later. Take the end across the top of the fixed end.

4 Gently and slowly pull the ends of the cord apart. You should see the shape of the knot beginning to form. Pull the knot until it begins to tighten. There will be at least one loop sticking out.

5 Turn the knot around and tighten the loops one at a time until all of the loops are snug and the knot is sufficiently tight and secure.

6 To move the knot, hold the cord on the side you want to move the knot toward, and push the cord into the knot. Observe which loop is linked to the cord that you pushed. Pull the loop until the knot is in the position you want. Turn the knot and tighten all the loops until the knot is snug. Always keep turning in the same direction. You will tighten each loop of the knot individually, through eight loops.

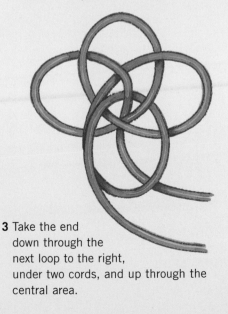

3 Take the end down through the next loop to the right, under two cords, and up through the central area.

sliding button loop

This knot can be used to create a decorative sliding knot for an adjustable necklace. The two ends of the cord overlap at the back of the necklace and a button knot is tied in each end. The knots are tied around the cord at the sides of the necklace and they may slide in either direction to change the length of the necklace. This is a more decorative variation of the simple sliding knot (see page 90).

1 Tie a button knot in one end of the cord, following steps 1–4 on pages 92–93. Be sure to observe where the central area of the knot is. Before you tighten the knot, thread the other cord, which forms the other end of the necklace, through the center of the knot.

2 Tighten the knot. Pull enough of the other end through to create another knot at the other end of the cord. This second knot has to be formed around the cord on the other side of the necklace, with the cord coming through the central area of the knot. As you create each loop, the part of the loop that goes up must go behind the cord at the side of the necklace, and the part that goes down must go in front of it.

3 Tighten the second knot. Clip the ends of both knots and secure with fray preventer or nail polish.

off-loom bead weaving

Off-loom bead weaving is very popular because of the great variety of things that can be made with nothing more than beads and a needle and thread. Off-loom weaving can mimic the ability of loom-woven beads to create flat-patterned fabric. But it can also go further by creating many structural and three-dimensional shapes too. It is possible to make beaded cords, toggles, clasps, buttons, balls, dolls, bowls, vases, and much more with off-loom weaving techniques.

comparing off-loom bead-weaving stitches

The table on the following pages compares many of the characteristics of different bead-weaving stitches, to help you select the appropriate stitch for your purpose. For example, if you are looking for a firm stitch to create the top of a tassel cap, you could look at the relative flexibility and rigidity of the different stitches and decide that a square or brick stitch may be most suitable for your needs.

There are exceptions to these guidelines. By working more than one stitch within a piece you can often achieve the qualities you want. The following pages explain the most commonly used off-loom bead-weaving stitches, how to increase and decrease them, how to work them into tubular cords, and a few other variations. Any of these stitches can be mixed together in one piece, they can be worked with differently sized and shaped beads, woven on top of a form, or many other variations to create endless possibilities.

	Can it be made with an odd or even number of beads?	Can different sizes and shapes of bead be used within the weaving?	Is the woven fabric flexible or rigid?
Peyote stitch	Even-count peyote stitch is easier. Odd-count peyote takes longer and requires a special edge on one side, which makes the weaving stiffer there.	Changes in bead size and shape need to be matched by increases and decreases in the fabric for the weaving to lie flat.	Moderately flexible. Can fold flat horizontally and curves around a small finger vertically.
Square stitch	Even and odd counts of beads are equally easy.	Changes in bead size and shape need to be matched by increases and decreases in the fabric for the weaving to lie flat.	More rigid than peyote. Suitable for building stable structures.
Brick stitch	Even and odd counts of beads are equally easy.	Changes in bead size and shape need to be matched by increases and decreases in the fabric for the weaving to lie flat.	The least flexible bead-weaving stitch. Excellent for building structures.
Netting stitch	Odd count is easier to make but even count can be formed by netting through pairs of beads rather than a single bead.	Can easily incorporate a variety of sizes and shapes of beads as the open spaces accommodate changes.	Extremely flexible due to the open spaces. Unsuitable for rigid structures but has excellent drape.
Right-angle weave	Even and odd counts of beads, in the base row, are equally easy.	Changes in bead size and shape can be incorporated without increases and decreases if they occur at the same place within the right-angle beading sequence.	Very flexible, but can be made firmer by passing the needle through the beads extra times, filling the holes with thread.
Herringbone weave	Must be made with an even number of beads.	Beads can change in size and shape from one row to the next and the work will still lie flat. In tubular herringbone weave, spiral effects can be created by using different-sized beads in each spine.	Quite rigid.
Chevron stitch	Any number of beads or units is possible.	Beads from one side of the weaving sequence can be a different size and shape from beads on other sides, and the units and fabric will still lie flat.	Naturally flexible due to the open spaces. By filling the bead holes with more or thicker threads it can be made more rigid.

Can it make a tubular structure like a necklace cord?	Can it be woven into a flat circle?	Is it useful for making beaded beads?	Is it strong enough for structural parts of jewelry?
Yes, makes an excellent tube.	Yes, excellent.	Yes, excellent. Best worked around a core bead.	Yes. Where it may receive a lot of wear, reinforce with extra passes of the needle and thread.
Yes, but more rigid than peyote.	No.	Only tubular beads, not rounded. No core bead needed.	Yes, very strong with many passes of the needle and thread.
Yes but very firm, with little drape.	Yes.	Only tubular beads, not rounded. No core bead needed.	Yes, but where the looped thread wraps around the other looped thread, it may need to be reinforced.
Yes, a variety of tubular shapes are possible.	Yes.	Yes, excellent but you may be able to see the base bead through the netting. Core bead essential.	Quite strong, but small areas may not support a lot of weight.
Can make tubes as well as tubular shapes with 3 sides.	Yes.	Excellent for beading beads. Core bead recommended.	Excellent.
Yes, makes an interesting variety of tubes, which are very firm and strong.	Can be worked in a circle but will make fluted, angular shapes.	Yes, but they will have angular shapes rather than rounded ones. No core bead needed.	Extremely strong. Can be made stronger by weaving down through an extra bead in each column. You will need to weave up one exra bead in the following column to complete the pattern.
Can form tubes. Single rows worked in some sequences make excellent "chains."	Can be worked in a circle but will make fluted, angular shapes.	Yes, but they will have angular shapes rather than rounded ones. Core bead optional.	Moderately strong, but can be made stronger by passing the needle and thread extra times through the beads.

STITCHING AND WEAVING

ladder stitch

Ladder stitch is used to create a foundation row on the edge of a piece of work, before some other weaving stitches begin. Follow the thread path in the diagram below. Ladder stitch can also be joined into a loop to begin weaving tubes in brick stitch or herringbone.

using a stopper bead

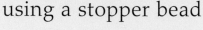

A stopper bead is an ordinary bead that prevents the beads from falling off the thread when there is no knot. It also helps to maintain tension while you are working. Use a bead in a different color so that you remember to remove it when the work is complete. Bring the needle through the stopper bead and back around through the same side again before beginning your work.

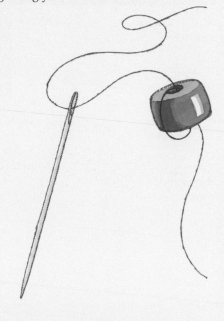

tip
When using a stopper bead, care must be taken to avoid splitting the thread with the needle. Pull the first loop of thread through the bead; hold it taut to one side of the bead as you carefully put the needle through on the other side of the bead. If the thread remains unpierced, the stopper bead can easily be worked off the weaving when the work is finished.

charting bead-weaving stitches

Many cross-stitch and knitting patterns can easily be converted for bead weaving. The graph papers on pages 238–249 will help you to chart patterns. Each stitch produces a different arrangement of beads, requiring a separate diagram to represent it. For example, in peyote stitch the beads lie in a horizontal castellated formation, while in square stitch they sit vertically one on top of another in straight columns.

It is helpful to use a clear plastic ruler when reading the charts. Place the ruler edge along the bottom of the bead row you are working and remember to use an arrow to mark the direction in which you are beading. Many stitches will require you to read the chart from left to right and then right to left, back and forth as you work your rows.

embellishing bead weaving

You can embellish any woven beadwork, including beaded buttons and beads as well as flat stitches. Embellishing is simply adding beads to the surface of the design that are not integral to the structure of the weave. A wide variety of beads and patterns can be used to create different looks: small or big loops, pyramid edging, bugle beads to make spikes, faceted beads to add sparkle, and drops or daggers to create bumps. The possibilities are endless.

tips

Thread color may show between beads, so try to match it to the color of the piece that you are embellishing. Bead loops can be as large as you like, but choose an odd number of beads. Embellishing is more vulnerable to wear and tear because it sticks out. If it is likely to receive a lot of wear, reinforce the beads with a second round of thread. If possible, use a doubled thread.

three-bead loop

Here the bead weaving is embellished by stitching through a base bead, adding three beads, and going back through the base bead in the same direction as the first time, creating a loop of beads around the base bead. This can be done randomly over the surface of the work or it can be done to every bead in one or more rows for a denser look.

five-bead loop

This embellishment uses the same principle as the three-bead loop but smaller beads may be used. Alternatively, use two smaller beads on either side of a large bead.

pearls

Here, a tiny button-shaped pearl is used in place of small beads. Try other interestingly shaped small beads, such as teardrops, magatamas, or sequins.

bugle-bead spikes

Bugle beads used in place of seed beads will stick straight up. Do not use bugle beads longer than 8 mm, because the work may be too vulnerable to snagging.

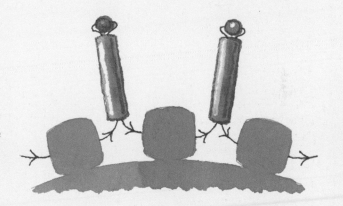

points

Spiky loops can be created by making a point with a small bead on top, then stringing through the second-to-last bead twice as shown in the illustration. To accentuate the spiky shape, make the loops between beads rather than on top of them, although this could create an interesting look too.

peyote stitch

Peyote stitch is the most commonly used bead-weaving stitch. It produces a flexible fabric. It is also sometimes known as one-drop and two-drop (which is a slight variation), or gourd stitch (when it is worked in the round or around a form). It can also be worked in a flat circle, known as circular peyote.

peyote stitch sample with
irregular contrast beads

peyote stitch sample with
stripes of contrasting beads

weaving flat peyote

Peyote stitch is worked differently at the edges, depending on whether it is constructed with an even or odd number of beads in each row (see opposite). It is easier to weave an even number of beads but sometimes an odd number is needed to place a motif in the exact center or to fit a form.

charting peyote stitch

Peyote stitch can be worked in many designs and is ideal for making charted patterns (see pages 238–249 for graph-paper charts to photocopy for making your own designs). When you begin picking up beads for the initial row, pick up the first bead from row 2, the first bead from row 1, the second bead from row 2, the second bead from row 1, and so on until you have threaded enough beads for the first and second rows.

Begin the weaving by picking up the last bead from row 3 (bead 7) and weaving through the last bead of row 2 (bead 5). Then pick up the next bead in row 3 (bead 8) and weave through row 2 (bead 3). Row 1 beads will fall into place between row 2 beads once the third row is complete.

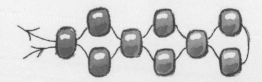

When working tubular peyote, the first bead of every row will move one bead to the left. When following a graph, use this diagonal line as a reference point.

even-count flat peyote

1 Make a foundation row by stringing an even number of beads, twice the number you want in one row. Pick up a new bead and bring your needle back through the second-to-last bead.

2 Pick up another bead, skip a bead in your foundation row, and go through the next bead up.

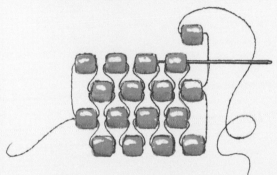

3 Continue like this to the end of the row. The beads in this row and the previous rows will fall into castellated lines.

odd-count flat peyote

On one side of the weaving, odd-count peyote uses the same simple turn used in even-count peyote shown at left. The other side requires a slightly more intricate turn that uses more passes of the needle.

1 Form an initial row, using an odd number of beads. There are nine beads in the illustration below.

2 Continue adding beads and weaving in the manner used for even-count peyote until you have added bead 13. Then bring your needle through beads 2 and 1, maintaining a firm tension.

3 Pick up bead 14 (the last bead of row 3) and weave through beads 2, 3, and 13 and back through 2, 1, and 14. This will bring your needle into the correct position for beginning the fourth row with bead 15. The right edge of your weaving will have a regular even-count turn and the left edge will require the needle to make this extra round each time in order to create the odd-count peyote edge.

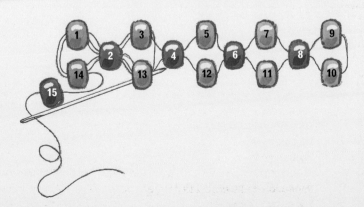

peyote increase on the edge

Increasing on the outside edge of peyote (as with most bead-weaving stitches) is straightforward. Simply add more beads after the end of a row.

To maintain an even-count peyote you will need to add enough beads for two extra columns as shown in the illustration. To make an odd-side increase by just one extra column you will be turning even-count peyote into odd-count peyote and will need to work the edge as instructed for odd-count peyote.

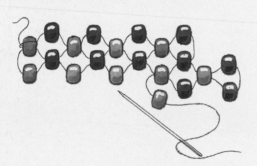

peyote increase in the middle

Sometimes you may want to increase within the fabric of the piece, for example when you are weaving on a form or in the round for a flat circular shape.

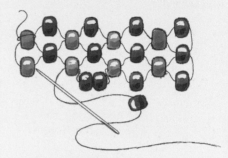

1 Pick up two beads instead of one where you wish your increase to occur and follow the usual peyote thread path.

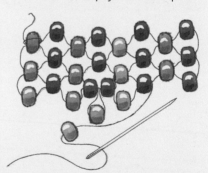

2 In the following row you will add a bead between these two new beads. Subsequent rows will be worked as usual.

peyote decrease

To decrease on the outside edges of peyote, simply leave off a bead. This will cause even-count peyote to become odd-count peyote and you will need to weave your needle through the work to bring it into the correct position to continue the next row.

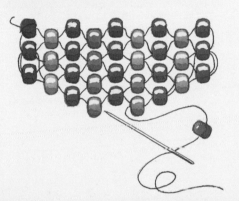

two-drop and three-drop peyote

Peyote stitch can also be worked with two or three beads at a time. This will make faster weaving and a more flexible fabric. However, it also means that designs will step up by two beads (or three) each time and edges will be castellated by two beads —advantageous in geometric designs.

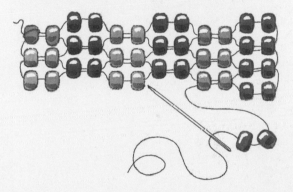

tips

To decrease peyote stitch in the middle of the weaving, simply pull two beads in a row together without inserting a bead between them. In the next row work these two beads as if they are one from the previous row.

Peyote stitch is an excellent bead-weaving stitch for covering irregular forms because the increases can be worked as the form suggests. For this reason, peyote stitch is also called gourd stitch because it is used to cover gourds with bead weaving.

flat circular peyote

Peyote stitch can be used to create flat or fluted round shapes. The exact number of bead increases needed around the circumference of the circle depends on the size and shape of the beads used. This example was worked in size 14⁰ beads.

1 Thread the needle with a long piece of conditioned nylon thread. Working with a single thread, string three beads and slide them 6 in (15 cm) from the end of the thread.

2 Tie the beads into a ring using a square knot (see page 89) and then pass the needle back through the first bead.

3 For row 2, pick up two beads in each space (six beads added). When you come to the end of this row, go down through a first-row bead and then up through two of the second-row beads.

4 Begin the third row by adding a bead, then going through the next second-row bead. Continue following the method for peyote stitch, working in circular rounds rather than rows.

tips

Generally, a rounded seed bead makes a smoother circle, but tubular seed beads can also be used for a more geometric effect.

Don't choose beads with tiny holes because the needle and thread will need to make repeated passes through them.

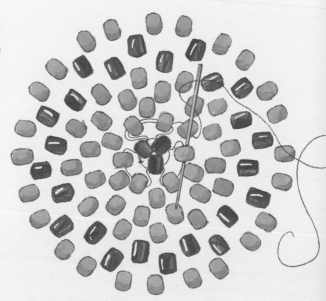

5 Continue as shown in the illustration, increasing to 12 beads in row 4 and to 24 beads in row 8.

STITCHING AND WEAVING

tubular peyote

Tubular peyote is best begun on a mandrel but it can be slipped off once the work is under way. A pencil or knitting needle makes a convenient mandrel for small peyote tubes. Alternatively, use a clear rubber tube to give a firm shape.

Working even-count tubular peyote is straightforward, but odd-count peyote will require a step up at the start of each row.

odd-count tubular peyote

Odd-count tubular peyote is worked in the same way as even-count tubular peyote, except there is a step-up at the beginning of each new row. Mark the beginning of the tube with a paper clip so that you know where this step-up occurs.

1 Thread a needle and string on an odd number of beads. The exact number will depend on the circumference of your tube and the size of your seed beads. There should be enough beads to fit around the circumference of your mandrel, leaving two or three bead widths of extra space. Slide the beads to within 15 cm (6 in) of the end of the thread.

2 Tie the thread ends together with a square knot (see page 89). Slip the ring of beads over the mandrel to support the work. The initial ring of beads will become rows 1 and 2 when the third row of beads is added, pulling the ring of beads into their up and down positions.

3 To start row 3, go through the first bead to the left of the knot, pick up a bead, skip a bead on the ring, and go through the next bead. Continue around until you are back where you started.

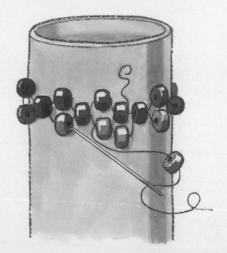

4 To begin row 4, pick up a bead and pass the needle through the first bead of row 3. Continue around until back at the beginning of the new row.

even-count tubular peyote

1 Thread a needle and string on an even number of beads. The exact number will depend on the circumference of your tube and the size of your seed beads. There should be enough beads to fit around the circumference of your mandrel, leaving two or three bead widths of extra space. Slide the beads to within 6 in (15 cm) of the end of the thread.

2 Tie the thread ends together with a square knot (see page 89). Slip the ring of beads over the mandrel to support the work. The initial ring of beads will become rows 1 and 2 when the third row of beads is added, pulling the ring of beads into their up and down positions.

3 Spread the beads so they are evenly spaced around the form. To start the next row, take the needle through the first bead to the left of the knot. Pick up a bead, skip a bead on the ring, and go through the next bead. Pull the thread down tight enough so that the bead you are adding pushes the bead above it halfway up the neighboring beads. Continue around until you are back where you started.

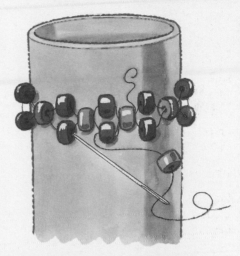

4 When ending row 3, pass the needle through the first bead of row 2 and the first bead of row 3. You are now ready to begin row 4. Each time you end a row, your needle will pass through the first bead of the preceding row and the first bead of the row you are working on.

tip
When working tubular peyote, the first bead of every row will move one bead to the left. When following a graph, use this diagonal line as a reference point.

square stitch

Square stitch produces a firm, strong fabric because each bead is worked through at least three times. The beads stack up directly, one above another, making it an easy stitch to use when following a pattern on graph paper. It can be worked by adding one, two, or three beads at a time. The one-bead version is the most common and is illustrated here.

one-bead square stitch

1 Begin by stringing a foundation row of beads of the length desired. Odd or even numbers are of no consequence.

2 For row 2, string two beads from left to right, and then pass the needle down through the second to last bead of row 1, from right to left. Come back up through bead 2 of the second row, passing the needle from left to right.

3 Continue by stringing one more bead in row 2, passing through the third-to-last bead of row 1 (from right to left), and back through the bead just strung, passing the needle from left to right.

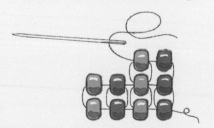

4 Repeat this looping technique across to the end of the row. The next row will be worked in the opposite direction.

> **tip**
> Square stitch makes a strong grid and can be worked in beads of any size and then embellished. Try working square stitch in a $6°$ or $8°$ seed bead with a thick nylon thread and then attaching beads on headpins to the thread work. Adding many short dangles to the beaded base can produce a shag-carpet effect.

increasing along outside edge

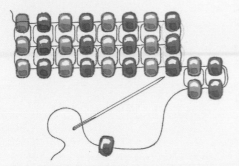

Increase along the outside edge by as many beads as needed, stringing the required number of beads at the end of a row and then working them into a square stitch with the beads of the next row as shown.

increasing inside the fabric

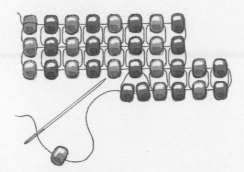

To increase in the middle of square-stitch weaving, add two beads instead of one. In the next row each of these beads will have one bead square stitched to it. This may cause the weaving to flare outward.

tip
By using different off-loom weaving stitches within the same fabric, you can make use of the advantages of different stitches to create stable, firm structures with beads lying in more than one direction. This is particularly useful when you want to explore beading shapes, such as beaded beads, or when you want to lend extra strength to an area of weaving, such as the joins.

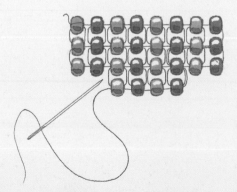

decreasing square stitch

Decrease on the outside edges of square
stitch by following the illustration at left.
To decrease within the fabric of square
stitch, simply skip over a bead in the row.

tubular square stitch

Tubular square stitch is best worked around an object such as a mandrel, because it is easier to start with something to hold its shape as you work.

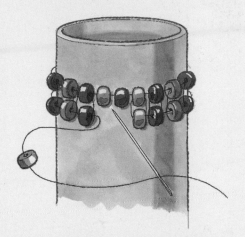

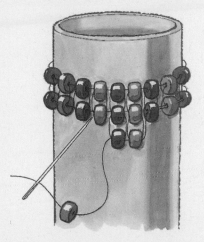

1 String on as many beads as you need to fit around the circumference. Tie them into a ring and slide them onto the mandrel. Pass the needle through the first bead in the loop to hide and bury the knot.

2 Do square stitch around the mandrel in the usual manner. When the row is finished, work back in the opposite direction to create the next row. Each row will be worked in the opposite direction of the one before.

brick stitch

Brick stitch is sometimes known as comanche weave. It makes a firm, strong, somewhat rigid fabric of staggered vertical beads. It is excellent for building structures such as the top of the tassel on the opposite page, which has then been embellished to give the top a fuller look.

weaving brick stitch

1 Begin with a foundation row of ladder stitch (see page 98). The number of beads in the foundation row will depend on how wide you want the weaving to be and the size of the beads.

2 To start row 2, string one bead and then pass through the closest exposed loop of the foundation row, holding your new bead in a vertical position while pulling the thread tight.

3 Pass back up through the same bead and continue, adding one bead at a time in this manner.

In the photo opposite, embellished loops of three beads were made through every bead in the brick stitch to fashion the full, acorn-shaped tassel top. Brick stitch provides the excellent firm structure, while the embellishing creates extra glitter from the many different directions that the light is reflected from the embellishing beads.

concealing thread

The thread that travels up the edge of each row can be concealed with a bead. Follow Step 1 for weaving brick stitch, then begin a second row. String two beads and then pass the thread through the closest exposed loop of the foundation row, holding your new beads in a vertical position while pulling the thread tight. Pass back up through the second bead and continue, adding one bead at a time in this manner.

increasing brick stitch

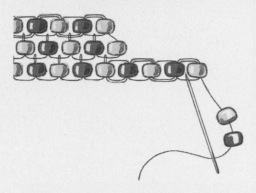

1 Increasing on the outside edge of brick stitch requires the addition of a bead ladder begun after the last bead of the row. Although it is possible to increase by just one bead at a time, the bead will have a tendency to curl inward.

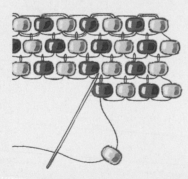

2 It is tidier to make single increases within the fabric, where the beads are forced to lie in the correct arrangement. To do this, simply work two beads into the loop of one of the previous rows.

decreasing brick stitch on the outer edge

To decrease brick stitch on the outer edge, begin adding beads on the next row between the second-to-last and third-to-last beads of the previous row, skipping over the last loop.

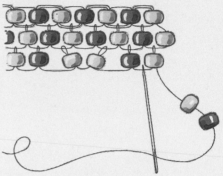

decreasing brick stitch in the middle

To make a decrease in the middle of the fabric, simply skip a loop and work into the next loop instead.

circular brick stitch

To begin, use any odd number of beads in the center. Three are used in this sequence but five would work equally well.

1 Make a slipknot (see page 89) with a 6 in (15 cm) tail of thread. Pick up one bead and pass the needle through the loop of the slipknot and back up into the same bead.

2 Add two more beads to the ring of thread in the same manner. Then carefully pull the tail of the slipknot to close the loop.

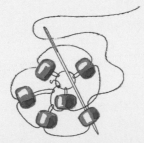

3 Bead 4 attaches to the thread on the outside of the first bead. Pick up bead 4, and then pass the needle under and over the thread and back into bead 4. Add another bead to that same thread to make an increase.

4 Continue working around, adding two beads to the threads that connect the previous row of beads. Row 2 will end up with six beads.

5 To make the circle lie flat, continue beading until the circle starts to cup and then add some increases to the next row. The beads will spiral around the center.

tubular brick stitch

Tubular brick stitch is best begun on a mandrel, but it can be slipped off once the work is under way. A pencil or knitting needle makes a convenient mandrel for small tubes.

1 Make a bead ladder the same length as the circumference of your mandrel (see page 98). Follow the instructions for weaving flat brick stitch (see page 114).

2 Join the two ends by looping the thread through the end beads. Pick up a bead and, moving to the right, loop around the connecting threads in the bead ladder.

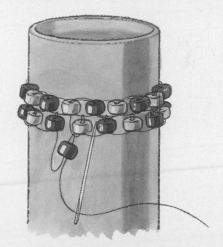

3 Continue the row in the same way. On reaching the end of the row, attach the next bead to the thread so that it is on the outside of the first bead of that row. Continue around the mandrel.

right-angle weave

Right-angle weave is the only construction method that sets the beads at right angles to each other. It produces a slightly open, flexible fabric. However, the fabric is more rigid than netting-stitch fabrics.

right-angle weave with four beads

Typically, four beads make up one unit of right-angle weave, but more can be used. For example, a unit of right-angle weave could consist of two beads on each side, making a total of eight beads. The illustration below uses four beads.

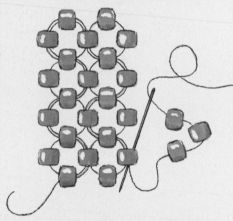

Start by threading and joining four beads in a circle. Add three beads in a figure-eight movement. For subsequent rows, add three beads for the first unit; then add two beads and work through two beads from previously constructed units.

increasing

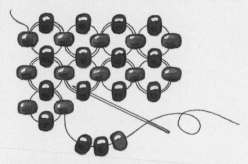

To increase right-angle weave, add extra beads to the bottom side of a unit. In the next row, these beads will be treated as if they are the bottom bead in two separate units.

decreasing

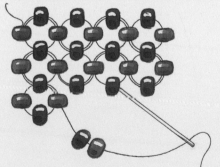

To decrease right-angle weave, skip a bottom bead in a unit from the previous row and begin weaving the next unit one bead over.

tubular right-angle weave

Tubular right-angle weave, with four or more units, is best begun on a mandrel, but it can be slipped off once the work is under way. A clear rubber tube can be used to keep the form rigid, or work through each of the beads until they are filled with thread to make it extra rigid.

1 Begin by making a ring of right-angle weave units (each consisting of four beads in the illustration) large enough to fit around the mandrel. Join them into a loop and slip onto the mandrel.

2 Begin row 2 by coming out of the bottom bead of a first-row unit (from right to left) and stringing three more beads. Go back through the bottom bead of the first-row unit from right to left.

3 Bring the needle down through the first of the strung beads in the new unit and string two more beads.

4 Bring the needle through the bottom bead in the next unit from left to right and then back down through the first-strung bead in row 2.

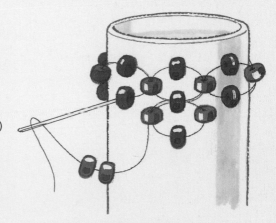

5 The needle will now go into the bottom bead in the new unit from right to left, back up the left-side bead, and right to left through the bottom bead in the next unit from the previous row. Continue in this figure-eight pattern.

herringbone weave

This stitch is also known as Ndebele (*en-de-BEL-ay*) after the African tribe which uses a similar technique in traditional bead weaving. The beginning row must have an even number of beads. Each pair of strung beads is referred to as a spine. The first row of beads is worked in a ladder stitch.

basic herringbone weave

1 Prepare a row of ladder stitch with an even number of beads (six in this example) with the needle exiting the top of bead 6.

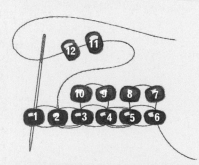

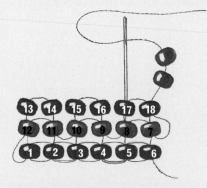

2 String two more beads, then bring the needle down through bead 5 and up through bead 4. String two more beads, then bring the needle down through bead 3 and up through bead 2. String two more beads, then bring the needle down through bead 1 and back up through bead 12.

3 Add two more beads and then go down through bead 11 and back up through bead 10. Continue this pattern, working back across the fabric.

4 A firmer and stronger version can be made by weaving down through the two previous rows of beads rather than just one. In this example, after adding beads 13 and 14, you would go down through bead 11 and 2, back up through 3 and 10, before adding beads 15 and 16.

increasing herringbone weave

Increases must always be made in pairs to keep the number of beads in each spine even. To make increases on the outside edges, add more pairs of beads and weave them as new spines.

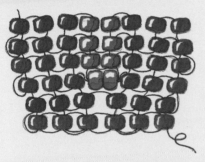

To make increases within the fabric, add pairs of beads between the two vertical herringbone beads. In subsequent rows, these form vertical beads for the edges of two spines.

herringbone decreases

To decrease, drop a spine at the edge of the fabric. This will make a stepped edge because you will be dropping two beads from the sequence, not just one.

tubular herringbone weave

When working herringbone weave into a tube, many interesting effects can be created by changing the size of beads in one or more spines. In the example below, if beads 1 and 2 are of a larger size they will spiral around the tube. This can be used to great effect if woven in a contrasting color as well. No mandrel is needed for a herringbone tube since it is very firm.

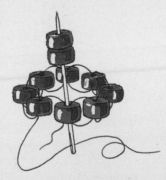

Work an even number of beads into a ladder-stitch loop. Continue weaving herringbone around the tube. When you go back down through the final bead in row 1, bring the needle back up two beads before you string two new beads.

netting stitches

Some people refer to any bead weaving that occurs off-loom as netting stitches. However, for the purposes of this book we will use the more commonly understood definition of netting stitch as a stitch that creates open spaces in the weave.

Netting stitches require fewer beads than other weaving stitches and are therefore lighter, faster to work, and drape beautifully. The open spaces in the weave can expand and contract the area they fit around. The size of the open spaces depends on the number of beads strung from the bead that is used to weave through. To graph a pattern, the number of beads in a net would need to be recorded on graph paper. The variations in number and size of bead are limitless, making this a difficult stitch to graph. Typically, the bead that is woven through is a different color, size, or shape from the other beads in the net.

Netting may be created by looping the working thread around a thread loop from a previous row (as in the helix rope on page 125) or through a bead from a previous row, as shown opposite.

tip
Because netting is an open stitch, it can be effective to work it around contrasting materials, such as a silk cord.

simple netting stitch

This example shows a netting stitch worked over an odd number of beads (in this case nine). An even number of beads can also be used; the needle would be inserted into the center two beads in each group instead of the middle one.

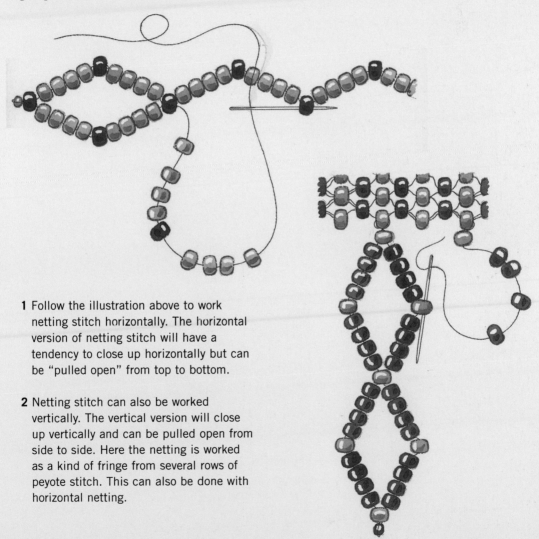

1 Follow the illustration above to work netting stitch horizontally. The horizontal version of netting stitch will have a tendency to close up horizontally but can be "pulled open" from top to bottom.

2 Netting stitch can also be worked vertically. The vertical version will close up vertically and can be pulled open from side to side. Here the netting is worked as a kind of fringe from several rows of peyote stitch. This can also be done with horizontal netting.

increasing netting stitch

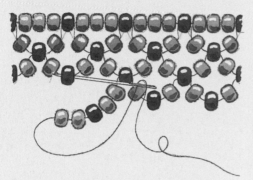

An increase can be made by changing the number of beads in a loop. An increase is formed by adding five beads where there were previously three.

decreasing netting stitch

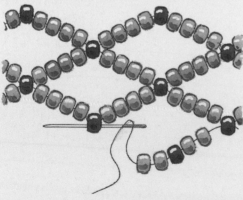

A decrease can also be made by changing the number of beads in a loop. A decrease is formed by adding five beads where there were previously nine.

tubular netting

Tubular netting is best done on a mandrel because it is so limp. If a firm tubular effect is required, a clear rubber tube can be used to create shape.

1 String on as many beads as you need to fit around the circumference of the mandrel. This example uses a number divisible by four, creating a center opening of three beads, which will expand to the odd number of five. Tie them into a ring and slide them onto the mandrel. Pass the needle through the first bead to hide the knot.

2 String five beads, skip three beads from row 1, and go into the fourth bead on the mandrel. Continue around the tube until you come back to the first bead in row 1.

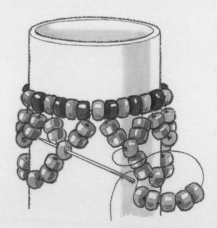

3 Pass through the first bead in row 1, then beads 1, 2, and 3 in row 2. Begin the next row of netting by stringing five beads and going through the center bead in the next group of five from row 2. Continue around the tube.

making a helix rope

Netting stitches can be created by working the thread in a loop around the thread loops between beads instead of through the beads themselves. This will produce an even softer drape and a more rounded shape to the netting. A common use for this technique is in making a helix rope.

The looping occurs in a different place throughout the beading, creating a spiral pattern. This effect can be used to good advantage by making one of the beads a different color or size. This will also make it easier to know where to loop your thread in the bead sequence.

The size of the beads and the number of beads in the initial ring will determine the diameter of the helix.

Helix ropes are best worked on a mandrel, because it is difficult to keep the loop in the right place without one. Use a pencil or knitting needle as a mandrel for creating small tubes.

1 String on four sets of four beads, with every fourth bead contrasting in color, size, or shape. Tie into a ring and slip onto the mandrel.

2 Pick up five beads (three main color, one contrast, one main), and loop the working thread between beads 4 and 5 in row 1. Continue around the ring, picking up five beads (three main, one contrast, one main) and looping the thread around the thread of the previous row after the next set of four beads. Keep the tension very tight so that the loops don't jump beads.

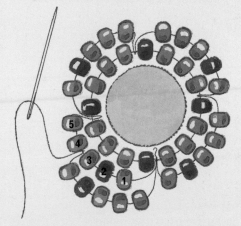

3 For the third and subsequent rows, pick up five beads (three main, one contrast, one main) and loop the needle around the thread between beads 3 and 4 of the previous row. Continue spiraling around until the desired length is reached.

chevron stitch

Chevron stitch is another stitch that creates open spaces in the weave, this time the characteristic V shapes. Vary the chevron by changing the bead count, shape, size, and color placement. Like netting stitches, the structure of this stitch varies a lot with changes in bead count, so each pattern requires a unique graph.

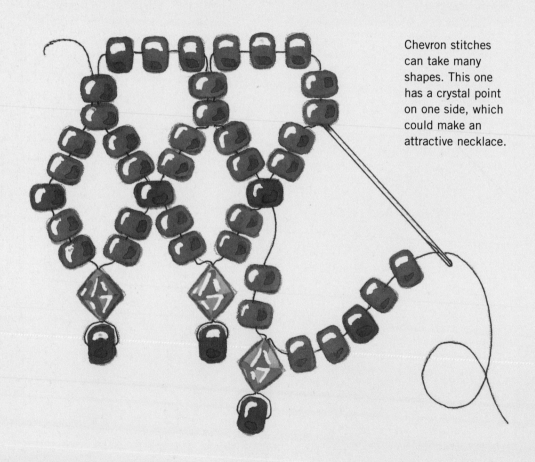

Chevron stitches can take many shapes. This one has a crystal point on one side, which could make an attractive necklace.

chevron chains

Use two colors of beads in this first sample to help you follow the correct beading sequence.

1 String one main-color bead and then loop through it again to make it into a starter bead. Leave a 6 in (15 cm) tail of thread. Add two more beads of the main color, one contrast, three main and three final contrast color beads, making a total of ten.

2 Pass the needle back through beads 1, 2, 3, and 4, being careful not to pierce the thread through the stopper bead.

4 In this way, rows of chevron chains can be woven on top of, or next to, one another to create a fabric. The contrasting beads that form the side of one row become the side for the adjoining row.

5 Weave the needle through the beads until it comes out facing up from a side bead (4 in the first illustration). Add three main-color beads, three contrasting beads, three main-color beads and go back down through the first added bead in the new row. Weave from top to bottom through the sequence of three contrasting beads along the side of the previous row, and then begin another unit in the chevron chain sequence, below the first.

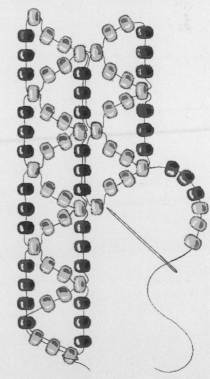

3 Pick up three contrasting beads (11, 12, and 13), and three main-color beads (14, 15, and 16), then pass the needle through bead 7. Pick up three more contrasting beads and three more main-color beads and pass the needle back through bead 14. Continue this technique until you reach the desired length.

loom work

Loom weaving with beads is very easy to do. Since the tension is mostly determined by the warp threads, it is possible to set up a bead-weaving loom for a child and then let them complete the weaving themselves with great success.

The long, vertical threads that support the work are called warp threads. The horizontal threads upon which you string the beads are called the weft or woof threads. The beads sit on top of each other in a grid with their holes aligned horizontally. This makes it an easy technique to chart on graph paper.

The finished fabric is strong and has a beautiful drape that is suitable for many things, including bags, necklaces, bracelets, and belts. Loom-woven beadwork can be embellished with any of the methods used to embellish off-loom work (see pages 100–101). It can also be completed with a fringe or edging (see pages 136–147) by finishing the warp threads off in this way.

the loom

A bead loom is much like a cloth loom. The warp threads, which support the work, are spaced a bead's length apart from one another by grooves on the upright partitions of the loom.

There are many styles and sizes of loom available. Smaller looms are suitable for weaving items such as bracelets and small amulet bags, while a longer loom is needed for items such as belts. More expensive looms are often designed with an adjustable length. Some looms are used upright, while others are designed to lie on a tabletop. They do the same thing; it's just a matter of personal comfort.

A small, inexpensive loom is suitable for the beginner to learn the techniques and experiment. Most of the smaller looms are designed for use with size 8°, 10°, or 11° seed beads. The threads are too widely spaced for beads smaller than 12°. For these beads you need to buy or construct a special loom.

Many people prefer to construct their own looms based on the needs of their projects. It is simple enough to do and instructions are widely available on the Internet.

choosing threads and needles

Warp threads will be slightly visible between the beads in the finished work, while weft threads will be visible along the edges (unless they are embellished). For this reason, choose a nylon beading thread, such as Nymo, in a color closest to your beadwork. When weaving beads of many colors, a neutral thread, such as gray or tan, can be a good choice. Choose gray if your beads have a cool undertone, such as blue, or tan if they have a warm undertone, such as red.

Nylon beading threads come in several sizes. The best choices for loomwork are A, 0, or 00, depending on the size of your beads. Each bead will have two weft threads plus up to three more thread ends running through it, so be sure your beads can accommodate four or five passes of the thread you choose.

calculating the warp

The number of threads used in the warp depends on the width of the piece of work. You will need one more thread than the number of beads. For example, a bracelet seven beads wide will require eight warp threads to be strung on the loom. The tension of the warp threads should be relatively tight. If you plan to bring the end of the piece of weaving to a one-bead point, you will need to string an even number of warp threads so the final bead is in the middle.

To calculate the length of the warps, add $3^1/4$–4 in (8–10 cm) minimum to each end of the piece of work. These bare ends will be used for sewing in and knotting of the warp threads or for making fringes. For example, an $7^1/4$ in (18 cm) bracelet will require warps of $13^3/4$ in (34 cm) or longer.

tips

Once loom work is under way, it cannot be removed until it is complete. For this reason, many bead weavers have more than one loom to work on.

To disguise the warp threads at the edges of bead weaving, embellish them with smaller beads. Suitable edging stitches are shown on pages 146–147.

threading the loom

To begin, tie the thread to the central hook or nail on one end of the loom, using an overhand knot (see page 88). Thread it in a groove (or the spring, if that is how your loom is made) at roughly the middle point, then take it straight down to the groove on the other end of the loom. Bring the thread over the grooved edge and around the hook or nail on the side, then back over the spring in the next groove to the left or right. Bring the warp thread back to the first end and through the adjacent groove.

Repeat as needed, spacing carefully and working an equal number of warp threads on either side of the first one. The warp threads on the outside edges of your weaving should be doubled for strength, as in the illustration below.

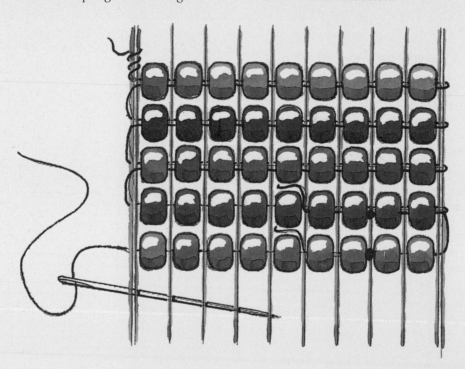

weaving

The weft threads are inserted between the warp threads with a needle and nylon thread. The following instructions are written for weaving from left to right; they reverse for weaving from right to left. This example is eight beads wide.

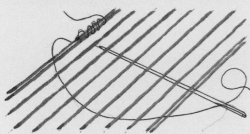

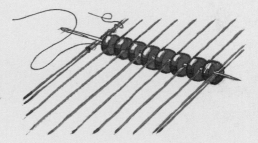

1 Thread the needle and tie off the end to the first (doubled) warp thread. Leave a 4 in (10 cm) tail to weave in and trim later. Weave this weft thread in and out of the doubled warp a few times to anchor it. Then bring the needle under all the warp threads to the other side so that you can start weaving from left to right.

2 Pick up eight beads on the needle. With your index finger under all the beads, push them up through the warp, making sure that a single bead fits between each pair of threads of the warp. Bring your needle through the beads.

3 Keep pushing the beads up, and re-insert the needle back through all the beads, over the tops of the warp threads. Be careful that you do not pierce the warp threads as you go back through (push the beads up higher, so that the needle is at the very bottom of the bead hole, if you have to).

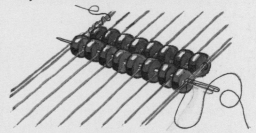

4 Bring the needle out of the beads and back under the warp. String on eight more beads and repeat until you have woven the length desired.

ending weft threads

As you weave you will come to the end of your weft thread and will need to securely knot and bury the ends of it before beginning a new thread.

1 When you come near the end of the thread, weave the thread back through a few beads of the previous row and then make a knot that incorporates a warp thread and both the weft threads.

2 Weave the thread through a few more beads and exit. Leave the trimming of thread ends until the work is finished. Loose ends will help to give you an idea of which beads have already been woven through an extra time.

adding new weft threads

1 To begin a new weft thread, leave a 4 in (10 cm) tail of thread and weave through two inside beads, one row above the new one to be started. After weaving through two beads, make a knot that incorporates a warp thread and both the weft threads.

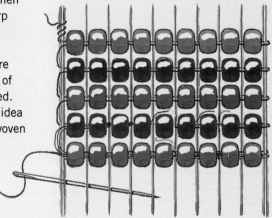

2 Follow the thread path until it exits on the left of the last completed row. Continue weaving. Leave the 4 in (10 cm) tail to be woven in when the work is complete.

increasing the width

Loom weaving can be increased and decreased along the outside edges only, not within the fabric of the weaving. Although this may look a little strange on the loom, as there will be many bare warp threads, these will be woven into the beads when the work is detached and will not be seen. All warp ends need to be woven in once the work is complete. For this reason, it is impossible for loom work to have staggered edges with many different points occurring along its edge, because the bare warp threads between the areas of beadwork would be too short to weave into the work. However, a single point along the length would be possible.

1 To add a bead on the left edge, bring the weft thread under the warp and back on top of it. Add a bead for the increase in the next row and work the thread back under the final warp thread.

2 Bring the needle through the first bead, and then bring the needle down under the second warp.

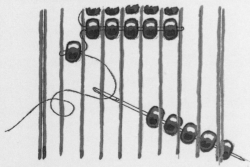

3 With the needle below the warp thread, pick up beads for the rest of the row and continue weaving.

decreasing the width

The top and bottom ends of loom weaving are often worked into a point or arch. In bracelets this is an elegant way to attach a closure finding. Follow these instructions to decrease into a point on the bottom edge of the weaving.

1 After the needle has passed back through a row of beads from right to left, bring the needle back under the final warp thread. Pass it through the number of beads by which you wish to decrease (one on each side in the diagram below).

2 With the needle under the new edge warp thread, bring it over the warp from right to left and then under from left to right.

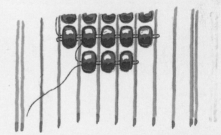

3 Continue adding the sufficient number of beads below the warp threads. To decrease on the right-hand side, add fewer beads than in the previous row. Bring your needle around to the top of the final warp thread and weave back through the beads as usual.

finishing warp threads

When the weaving is complete, double-check it to make sure every bead has been woven correctly. To remove it from the loom, snip the warp threads next to the nails or hooks at each end of the loom. You should have sufficient length of warp thread ends to weave back into the work or to make fringe.

Many loom-worked pieces have dramatic fringing at the bottom edge, and the warp ends provide an ideal opportunity for this. To turn warp thread ends into fringe, follow the basic instructions for creating fringe on pages 138–139. Keep in mind that you may need long lengths of warp ends to make fringe, so plan for this at the design stage before warping the loom.

Fringe can be plotted on graph paper and may be arranged in different colors or staggered lengths. The ends will still need to be woven back up into the main body of the beading and finished.

weaving in warp thread ends on a straight edge

It is usually impossible to hide all warp ends by burying them in the first row of weaving and, even if it were, this row would become stiff with thread work. It is better to distribute the warp ends throughout the bead weaving. A shorter Sharp needle is better for weaving in ends than a beading needle. Before you start, plan how you will go about weaving in the warp ends to avoid having them all clustered in the same row.

1 Begin by threading a needle with a warp thread somewhere in the middle of your weaving. Take the thread up four rows by weaving it over and under the weft threads.

2 Bring the warp thread through two beads, to the left or right, then tie and knot it around the warp and weft threads. Weave the thread through two more beads, then leave the end to trim when all the weaving is complete.

3 Continue with the other warp threads, distributing them evenly over the work. Knot and bury the threads in different rows from those previously buried.

weaving in warp thread ends on a pointed edge

1 Begin by threading one of the warp ends next to the final bead onto a needle. Weave the first warp up a row and insert the needle through one or more beads. Bring the needle up to the next row and weave the needle through several of the beads. Repeat this for the following row, weaving through two beads.

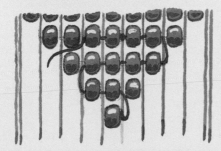

2 Make a knot to include the warp and both weft threads. Weave the needle through two more beads. Leave the end until all the weaving is complete before snipping.

tip

If there are many weft ends to weave in at a point, consider switching to a finer weft thread before you begin weaving in this area. For example, you could switch from a Nymo D to a Nymo B a couple of rows before the point is formed.

beaded fringe and edgings

Beaded fringe can be added to bead weaving or to any sort of fabric. Many different designs are possible by altering the size, shape, pattern, and color of the beads as well as the shape and style of the fringe. This section offers a few variations but experimentation will lead to many more. It can be helpful to plot your fringe design onto a graph before beginning to work.

The edges of woven beadwork usually show the beading threads. This is especially true for loom weaving where there is a doubled warp thread as well as weft loops at the edges. Embellishing the edges of bead weaving can conceal these threads, strengthen the weaving, and prevent edge threads from snagging.

fringe

Since it hangs away from the fabric and moves around, a beaded fringe is in danger of getting snagged. To avoid damage, make sure that the beads hang on the beading thread with no slack.

tips

It is a good idea to condition thread with a thread conditioner before beginning the fringe, to prevent tangles and help maintain an even tension.

Don't be tempted to work with lengths of thread longer than 1 yd (1 m). Although it may appear to save time in starting new threads and sewing in ends, you are much more likely to end up with frustrating tangles and knots.

Bare thread is more likely to snag than beaded thread. However, it is important not to thread the fringe so tightly that it is stiff and doesn't swing freely.

The beading thread must be securely anchored in the weaving or to the twill tape before you begin to thread the fringe. The fringe should also be secured with knots regularly to prevent accidents and ensure the ideal tension remains along its whole length.

Use the strongest available beading thread for the size of the beads used in the fringe. The thread will need to pass through each bead in the fringe at least twice and if the fringe is added to bead weaving, through the bead weaving as well (through beads that already have two or more passes of thread). Doubled thread can be used. Try a nylon beading thread, such as Nymo in size D, or a heavier waxed nylon thread for best results. Use a long beading needle and as long a length of thread as can be managed, about 1 yd (approximately 1 m) should do.

adding beaded fringe

1 To make fringe, secure a long thread in the bead weaving by weaving through several beads and making a knot around the existing threads in the weaving.

2 Weave the needle into place to start the fringe. If the beads in the weaving lie with their holes horizontally, as they do in peyote or square stitch, you will need to come out one side of the bead to begin the weaving. To finish the fringe strand you will go into the hole of the next bead. If the bead holes are vertical, as they are in herringbone stitch, come out the bottom of a bead. You will go back up into it to complete the fringe strand.

3 String on the beads to make up one strand of the fringe. These can be patterned with different colors, shapes, or sizes of beads.

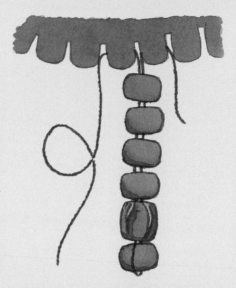

4 When you have woven through the last bead, pass the needle back up through all but the last bead and bring your thread back up into the bead weaving. The final bead holds the entire length of beads on.

5 Now bring the needle through the next bead in the weaving and make another strand of the fringe in the same way. You may wish to make a knot buried in the weaving after every strand or every couple of strands to help maintain tension across the fringe.

looped fringe

Fringe can also be created from loops of threaded beads along the edge of the woven beadwork or fabric. The loops can weave in and out of the same bead on the woven beadwork, or the two ends can be spaced apart by several edge beads.

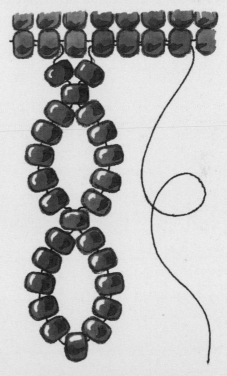

1 The fringe is worked doubled with the thread passing through different beads on the way back up to the edge of the woven beadwork. Be careful when doing this to keep the same length of beads on each side. Many beads have irregular sizes, and an equal count will not necessarily result in an equal length.

2 Create decorative loops by passing through a common bead on each side of the fringe strand. This is different from netted fringe, where each of the fringe strands is connected to the strands on either side. Here the looped fringes are spaced apart by several beads.

adding beaded fringe to fabric

Beaded fringes look great on the fabric hems of items such as curtains, scarves, or dresses. It is best to add the fringe to twill tape or some other ribbon and then stitch it in place behind the hem of the item. The twill tape will add extra strength and conceal the stitching.

Follow the suggestions on page 136 for choosing a thread to create a beaded fringe on fabric. With fabric you have the advantage of not having to fit the thread through the holes of the beads in the weaving so you should have greater opportunity to use a strong thread.

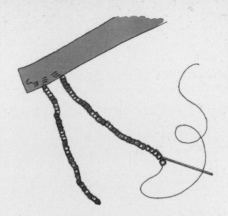

1 Cut a piece of twill tape to the desired length of the fringe. Leave an extra 3/4 in (2 cm) at either end of the tape for turning the edges under later.

2 You may want to use chalk to mark regular intervals on the twill tape before beginning. Try 3/8 in (1 cm) intervals unless your beads are very big or small. Adjust accordingly.

3 Thread a needle with beading thread, using it doubled if possible. Stitch and backstitch to secure it to one end of the twill tape.

4 Pick up the number of beads to give the desired length of the fringe strand. Push the needle back through the second-to-last bead and up through all the beads, bringing it out of the twill tape. Pull the thread to ensure it is taut but not too tight. Make several stitches to secure in place. Repeat for each strand of the fringe.

5 To stitch the twill tape to the hem of the fabric, complete the stitching of the hem first, concealing the raw edges. Tack the fringing to the wrong side of the fabric hem, placing the beaded edge of the tape about 3/8 in (1 cm) above the bottom edge. Topstitch or blindstitch the twill tape in place.

fringe variations

There are many variations possible for fringe and their endings. The examples below suggest some of the possibilities.

large bead ending

A heavier bead makes a good fringe ending because its extra weight adds more movement. Keep in mind the weight of the overall fringe when designing with larger beads. Will the piece support it? If it is a short fringe, such as a necklace, it will probably be fine, but if it is a long fringe, such as on a shawl hem, it might be too heavy.

simple loop ending

Instead of using just one bead at the end of each strand of a fringe, three may be used to form a small simple loop.

pearls and crystals

Pearls and crystal beads can be alternated to create a charming fringe.

large loop ending

A loop at the end of an interesting bead, such as a pearl, is a good way to add weight and length to a fringe. The loop can be as long as you like but odd numbers work best.

star bead ending

This star bead could end a fringe with just one seed bead or with a small loop, as shown here.

daisy chains

There are many variations on the daisy chain that make an excellent fringe. These can be woven for every strand of fringe or at regular intervals in a contrasting color from the rest of the fringe.

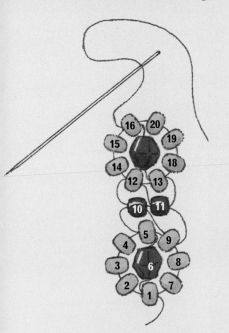

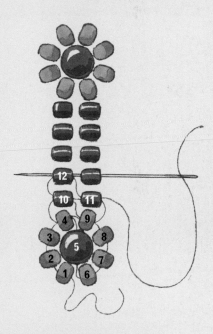

This daisy chain is separated by a two-bead link (beads 10 and 11) which may be made in another color so that the daisies are more obvious. Follow the numbered thread path: 1, 2, 3, 4, 5, 6, 1, 7, 8, 9, 5, 10, 9, 11, 10, 12, 11, 13, 12, 14, 15, 16, 17, 13, 18, 19, 20, 16.

A single daisy can also make a nice ending for a fringe. Simply work the thread exiting bead 7 back up beads 8, 9, 10, 5 and back up through the fringe.

The ten-bead-link daisy chain is a faster version of the full daisy chain. Each daisy is separated by links of ten beads and the central bead in the daisy is slightly larger. Use a contrasting color to make the bead petals of the flower. Follow the numbered thread path: 1, 2, 3, 4, 5, 6, 7, 8, 9, 10, 4, 9, 11, 10, 12, 11.

netted fringe

branched fringe

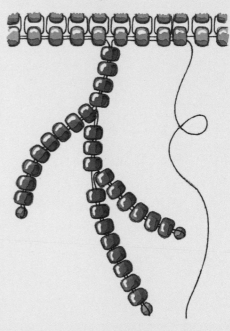

Netting stitch (see page 123) can be worked from the edge of bead weaving to form a fringe. To give the fringe weight and movement, try ending with a three-bead loop, with heavier beads, or with clusters of beads.

Beaded fringe can be worked with branches by following the illustration above. Flower- or leaf-shaped beads can be worked at or near the ends to extend the branch theme. A cluster of fringe strands in this method will make a very full and three-dimensional edging. This can also be worked as an embellishment on the surface of bead weaving.

twisted fringe

A twisted fringe is worked with each strand being a doubled length of beads that is encouraged to twist back on itself.

1 Place enough beads on the thread to equal twice the length of the fringe you desire. Lay the bead weaving down and grasp the thread next to the beads between the thumb and index finger of your right hand (opposite for left-handers). Twist the thread away from your body by sliding your thumb up your index finger.

2 To reposition your grip, hold the thread with the left hand. Repeat the motions until the thread twists back on itself.

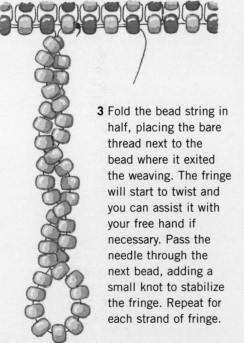

3 Fold the bead string in half, placing the bare thread next to the bead where it exited the weaving. The fringe will start to twist and you can assist it with your free hand if necessary. Pass the needle through the next bead, adding a small knot to stabilize the fringe. Repeat for each strand of fringe.

kinked fringe

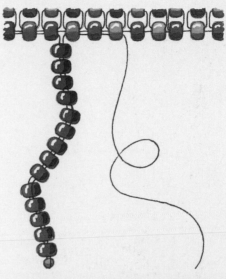

Fringe can kink in shape by excluding beads from the return pass of the thread. This makes a very three-dimensional fringe. In this illustration, the fifth and tenth beads from the top do not have the thread going back through them; it passes around the outside of the beads instead, creating extra tension and kinking the fringe.

edgings

The edges of woven beadwork usually show the beading threads. This is especially true for loom weaving, where there is a doubled warp thread as well as weft loops at the edges of the weaving. Embellishing the edges of bead weaving decorates and conceals the threads, strengthens the weaving, and prevents the edge threads from snagging.

All edging stitches are forms of embellishment since they do not contribute to the structure of the main fabric. But in some cases, such as right-angle weave, they can change the nature of the weaving. Right-angle-weave fabric left without edge embellishment can be quite floppy. However, if beads are added between the right-angle units, the fabric will be much firmer.

edgings for peyote and brick stitch

The edges of peyote and brick stitch are castellated. A three-bead picot or a single smaller bead makes a good edge embellishment for both these woven fabrics. Weave in and out of the edge threads, adding beads in loops.

edging for right-angle weave

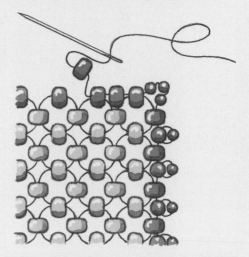

The weaving will usually require a smaller bead to fit between the vertical units and a larger bead between the horizontal units, but this will depend on the type and size of beads used in the original fabric. In this example of a right-angle edging, the vertical units are embellished with two sizes of smaller seed beads to form a picot edging. The horizontal units have the same-size bead as the main fabric woven between the horizontal beads in the unit. The corners have a three-bead picot in a smaller bead size.

edgings for square stitch or loom weaving

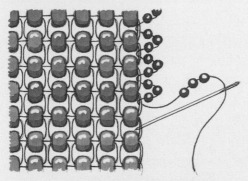

Square stitch or loom-woven fabric can be edged with a single bead, or with groups of three, next to each edge bead. The beads should be one size smaller than the main fabric beads. Round seed beads work well. The thread is woven in and out of the side loops, adding one or three beads each time.

edging for chevron stitch

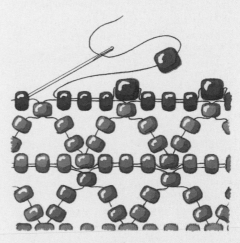

Chevron stitch is another weave, like right-angle, that will be firmer and stronger when edge beads are added. In this example one larger bead is added between the chevron sets.

bead embroidery

Beads can embellish many items made from other materials and can be attached in many different ways. One option is to stick them onto the object with glue or wax. The Huichol Indians in Mexico create beautiful bead mosaics by carving gourds, embedding them with wax, and then pressing seed beads, holes facing up, into the wax. However, embroidery offers perhaps the greatest opportunity for embellishing items with beads. Bead embroidery can be done on fabric, paper, leather, or any material that can be sewn through.

base fabrics and interfacings

Any material that will let a sewing needle pass through it can accept bead embroidery. The qualities of the fabric may change though. For instance, a knit fabric may lose its stretch unless an elastic beading thread is used. However, this can be used to your advantage to create a puckered fabric. If the elastic threads are used under tension, the beaded areas of a knit fabric will pucker together to create an interesting effect. If you are trying to avoid puckering, use an embroidery hoop or frame and a backing paper.

If you are embroidering a fragile material, such as handmade paper, you may wish to add a light, fusible fabric interfacing to the back of the paper to prevent tearing. This can be done before or after the bead embroidery. If it is done after the embroidery, it will also hide and stabilize the stitches on the back of the paper. Use a medium-low iron setting to adhere the interfacing to the paper.

Backing papers add a degree of stability to embroidered work. It is not necessary to attach one to the fabric back for a design that uses occasional beads, but for an allover beaded motif it will make the embroidery much easier. Backing papers can be found at fabric stores carrying embroidery supplies. Papers made for backing machine embroidery are suitable. Use a running stitch to attach the backing paper to the back of the fabric after mounting it in a hoop or frame. The stitches will be removed when the work is complete and the paper will either be dissolved or torn away, depending on the manufacturer's instructions.

tip
For an allover bead embroidery, use some kind of embroidery hoop or frame. Keep the frame tension loose; it is just meant to hold the fabric, not to stretch it.

beads for embroidery

Just about any beads can be used in bead embroidery. The most commonly used are basic Japanese or Czech 11° seed beads as well as smaller charlottes and other tiny beads. Larger beads with surface patterns and textures, such as Czech pressed-glass leaf beads, flat flowers, rose montees, and nail heads, can be used as secondary design elements.

Some designs are created around a large central bead, shisha mirror, or cabochon. Cabochons are usually glued to the backing with tacky fabric glue.

choosing a thread

The thread will not be as visible as it is in conventional embroidery, so regular nylon beading threads are the most suitable, in size D if possible. When sewing beads on fabric, don't wax the thread or use conditioner because they attract dirt.

Invisible thread is also useful for bead embroidery. This is a lighter thread than the standard fishing line used in beading and can be found with embroidery supplies in fabric stores. Invisible thread can be used to stitch sequins in place without a top bead and it will barely be visible. Make a stitch up through the middle of the sequin and over one side. Come up through the sequin again and over the opposite side.

embroidery stitches used in beading

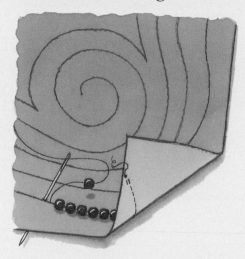

Unlike conventional thread embroidery, there are few actual stitches used in bead embroidery. In most cases, it is the beads that stand out, not the threads. However, the patterns of the beads are noticeable. These may be parallel, spiral, meandering, or other geometric shapes. These shapes will be more obvious with longer beads, such as bugles or Japanese beads, than with round seed beads. Plan your lines of stitching before beginning. To begin embroidering, always make a knot in the thread on the wrong side of the fabric and make a few backstitches to be sure the thread will hold.

couching stitch

Couching is one of the most practical methods of sewing seed beads and other small beads in place. It can be used to attach a row of aligned beads, which is helpful when creating shapes with the pattern of your bead embroidery. It can also be done with a decorative thread that will not fit through your beads. String the beads on a beading thread and then couch in place with your alternative thread or cord.

1 Work with two needles of thread. Bring the first strand up where you wish to begin beading and string on all the beads for couching. Position the first few beads where you want them to lie on the fabric.

2 Bring the second needle up through the fabric next to the end of your first bead. Take a stitch over the thread between the first and second bead.

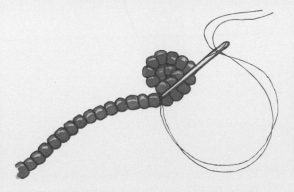

3 Bring the needle back up through the material and sew the row of beads down to the material by stitching over the thread between each of the beads. This will hold the beads in place.

single bead and sequin stitching

This stitch is useful for adding a single bead (larger than a seed bead) or to stitch sequins in place without invisible thread. It will create a raised surface since there will be a seed bead sitting on top of the bead or sequin.

Bring the thread up from the back of the fabric through the hole of a single bead or sequin. Attach it to the fabric by adding a single seed bead to the thread, then stitching back through the larger bead or sequin to secure.

stitching nail heads and rose montees

Nail heads and rose montees have flat backs and holes running parallel to the bead front. These are designed especially for bead embroidery. Although they are more commonly associated with vintage clothing, newer ones can still be purchased. They usually have holes running across the back in a crisscross pattern, so they can be stitched to the fabric at four junctions and will not move once in place.

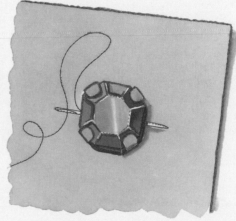

backstitch

Backstitch is used a great deal in bead embroidery. It is useful for stitching seed and small beads to fabric and makes a very strong stitch that will hold up well over time. If the beads are smaller (14°), you may string up to five at a time.

1 Bring the needle up through the fabric from the back. Then add three beads to the thread.

2 Stitch these three beads to the surface of the fabric. Be careful to reinsert your needle at a length just $1/32$ in (1 mm) longer than the length of beads to be attached.

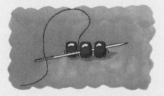

3 Bring the needle back up through the fabric near the second bead. Run the needle through the second and third beads, pulling them taut.

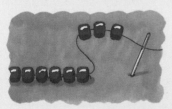

4 After exiting the third bead, add three more beads to the thread and stitch these down to the fabric. Repeat by bringing the needle up next to the second bead of the second set of beads. Continue the stitch for the desired length.

attaching shisha mirrors

Shisha mirrors are shapes made of mirror or other reflective materials and are frequently used in Indian embroidery to add shimmer. Although this method does not include beads, shisha mirrors are often used in beadwork.

1 Make a straight stitch across one side of the mirror, bring the needle up a little above the mirror, and make another straight stitch down one side.

2 Work a square of straight stitches, then another square on top in the same way, but across the corners of the previous square. These foundation stitches need to be tight and not too close to the edge of the mirror.

3 Bring the needle up next to the mirror and pass it under the foundation stitches, keeping the thread under the point of the needle (as though it were a blanket stitch). Pull tight.

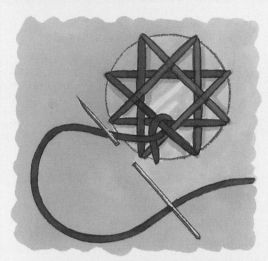

tip

When working embroideries that include large elements like shisha mirrors, add these first and then draw in or work the smaller bead designs around them. It is easier to work out how much space they take up this way.

4 Make a small stitch into the fabric, alongside the mirror, again keeping the working thread under the needle (like a chain stitch).

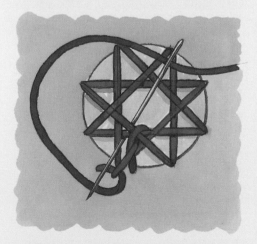

6 Make another small stitch into the fabric, inserting the needle into the previous "chain" stitch.

7 Repeat steps 5 and 6 all around the mirror and then knot the thread securely on the back.

5 Pass the needle under the foundation threads, keeping the working thread under the needle.

knitting and crocheting with beads

Beads can be included in knitted and crocheted fabrics. They can embellish the surfaces, trim the edges, or encrust the entire surface to make a new fabric, as in beaded crochet ropes. This section explains the specific methods of using beads in these techniques. You should already know how to knit or crochet before beginning to include beads. If you would like to learn these techniques, practice them from books on the subject in plain simple stitches before you begin with beads.

choosing beads

Seed beads in 8°, 6°, and 5° are the best sizes for bead knitting and crochet because their large holes make them easy to string. Smaller beads can be used, but they require finer threads and smaller needles. Cylindrical 11° seed beads can also be used because they have generous holes.

Cubes, triangles, teardrops, daggers, and fiber-optic beads are also a good choice because they are all light and small. Beads larger than 8 mm will usually be too heavy unless they are confined to just occasional placement.

tip
If you run out of beads while knitting or crocheting, cut off the thread and knot it to keep your work from unraveling. String more beads onto a new thread, tie it in as if joining a new yarn, and continue. Weave or stitch both loose thread ends to the wrong side and through several stitches or beads to secure. Clip the tail close to the work.

choosing yarn

Any yarn that can be strung with beads can be used in bead knitting or crochet. You can even add small, delicate beads to fabrics made with thicker yarns by carrying a second thinner yarn, threaded with beads, along with the work. Either knit or crochet with both yarns at the same time, or slip the finer one across the wrong side of the work when it is not needed. When the beads are required, push one down into the stitch and knit or crochet with both yarns.

When knitting or crocheting with allover beads, the yarn will act as a support more than a feature in itself. Choose a strong, smooth, tightly plied thread, such as polyester upholstery thread or mercerized crochet cotton. Both of these threads come in a variety of colors (including variegated ranges) and several sizes.

In thread sizes, the higher the number, the finer the yarn. A size 10 cotton crochet thread with a 1.25 mm (US 10) crochet hook and 6° beads is a good choice for beginners to learn the techniques.

preparing yarn

You will need to make an estimate of how many beads to string before you begin, since all stringing must be done before you begin to knit or crochet.

Always string beads with the yarn still on the spool, since you will use a lot more yarn than the length of beads. String the beads, then wind everything back onto the spool when you have finished.

It is easier to estimate the number of beads needed when you are working a plain fabric rather than a tube, because you can work out the number of beads based on the number of stitches in a row that will include them. However, it can be counterproductive to count each one if you have a lot to string because it is easy to lose count or make a mistake. It is better to make an educated guess and then round up. However, if you are following a beaded color sequence you will need to count them out accurately.

using wire

Wire is an interesting choice of material for bead knitting and crocheting. Wire will form a rigid structure with a very open framework to display the beads. The technique is usually done with knitting, but can also be crocheted or French knitted. A .3 mm or .2 mm (28- or 32-gauge) copper wire is usually used. These are available in a variety of attractive colors. If the wire is too fine it will snap, so make a sample piece before you begin your jewelry.

stringing beads on yarn

There are several ways to thread beads onto yarn and the approach taken will depend on the size of the yarn and beads. The most straightforward method is to use a big-eye needle. This is a long beading needle with a central split that makes threading it very easy. It is suitable for beads larger than 8° and some smaller beads with large holes.

If using a thicker yarn or larger beads you will need to follow one of the methods below. You can use a 2 in (5 cm) long folded piece of fine wire by laying the end of the yarn across it and then bending the wire in half. Twist the two ends of wire together and string the beads.

Bead spinners help make stringing random beads much quicker. They work by using a special curved needle in a bowl to quickly scoop up beads as they spin around. They are not very useful if you want to string a pattern of different colors or sizes of beads since they pick up whatever is in the bowl, making it hard to select what goes on when.

knitting with beads

A few beads or sequins can be sewn onto a finished piece of knitting, but if many are required and if they are to be placed evenly over part or all of the fabric, they should be knitted in, using one of the methods shown below.

The simpler of the two methods for knitting with beads or sequins is the slip-stitch method. The yarn-around-needle method must, however, be used where beads are to be worked into consecutive stitches. Keeping the beads on the right side of the work requires a little more skill than in the slip-stitch method. The beads or sequins can be worked into the knit side or purl side of the work. On the wrong side, work fairly tightly to hold the beads in place.

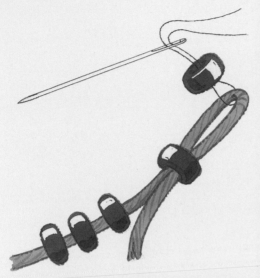

You can also use a thread loop to thread beads by first threading a sewing needle with a double strand of strong thread. Slip the end of the beading yarn through the loop of thread and turn back the end. Then string the beads or sequins onto the yarn. Always keep one bead on the loop to hold it in place. Continue stringing beads until you are finished and then push them back onto the yarn and undo the loops.

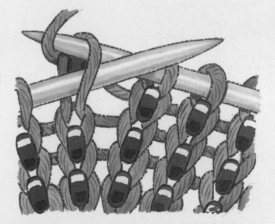

This knitted fabric includes allover bead placement. The best method for including beads throughout knitted and crocheted pieces is to work them in as you go along rather than sewing them in afterward.

slip-stitch method

This method can be used wherever the beads or sequins are separated by at least one stitch. It is normally worked on right-side rows, but can also be worked from the wrong side. At least two rows of knitting should be completed before beads are worked in.

slip stitch worked from the knit side of fabric

Knit up to the position for the bead. Bring the yarn forward and push the bead up next to the knitting. Slip the next stitch knitwise. Keep the bead in front of the slipped stitch, take the yarn to the back of the work, and knit the next stitch.

slip stitch worked from the purl side of fabric

If working a purl-side row when it comes time to add a bead, take the yarn back to the knit side of the work and slip the next stitch purlwise. Push the bead up so it lies close to the right side of the knitting, take the yarn to the purl side of the work, and purl the next stitch.

yarn-around-needle method

This is a little trickier to work than the slip-stitch method but has the advantage of including the beads in the actual knit stitches. This is useful if the beaded motif is larger than six consecutive stitches wide, where the slip-stitch method cannot be used.

1 On a right-side (knit) row, insert the needle through the back of the next stitch and push a bead up close to the work.

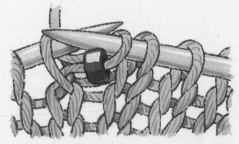

2 Take the yarn around the needle, and push the bead through the stitch to the front. Complete the stitch.

3 On a wrong-side (purl) row, insert the needle purlwise through the back of the loop. Take the yarn around the needle and complete the stitch, pushing the bead through the loop.

crocheting with beads

As with knitting, crochet can be a good way to work beads all over a fabric surface. The stitches used are usually the most basic—chain stitch, slip stitch and single crochet—but can be combined with more decorative crochet stitches.

When crocheting with beads, they will appear on only one side of the fabric in each row. To have them appear on both sides of the fabric, work them in every row. If you want them to appear only on the right side, work them in every other row. Either side of the fabric can be the right side, so mark with a safety pin the one you will use.

chain stitch with beads

Chain stitch is usually abbreviated in patterns as (ch). See the Appendix on page 251 for a complete set of crochet stitch descriptions.

To add beads to a chain stitch, begin by stringing your beads as described on pages 158–159. Slide a bead down the working yarn; then make a yarn over. Pull the yarn over through the chain loop. Continue for each bead you wish to place in a chain.

slip stitch with beads

Slip stitch is usually abbreviated in patterns as (sl st). Slip stitch can be used to crochet fabric or make a row of crochet into a loop.

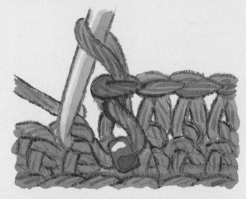

1 Bring one of the threaded beads down to the base of the yarn. Insert the hook from front to back through the top loop or loops of the single crochet of the previous row.

2 Bring the yarn over the hook and draw it through all the loops on the hook. You will be left with a single loop.

single crochet stitch with beads

Single crochet stitch is usually abbreviated in patterns as (sc). For a complete list of crochet stitch definitions and abbreviations see the Appendix on page 251.

1 Bring one of the threaded beads down to the base of yarn. Insert the hook from front to back through the top loop or loops of the single crochet on the previous row.

2 Bring the yarn over the hook and draw it through the single crochet loops with the hook facing you.

3 You have two loops on your hook; bring the yarn over the hook, and draw the hook through both loops. One loop remains on the hook.

crochet ropes

Including beads in every stitch of a circular crochet makes an elegant crochet rope. These can be used as necklaces or bangles. They drape beautifully and can be made in many patterns if the beads are strung in a sequence before work is under way. Ropes can be made in any diameter; the most common have 5 to 12 beads around.

Most ropes are made with a chain foundation and then slip-stitched or single-crocheted every stitch with a bead in a continuing spiral.

The table below is an estimate of how many beads to string for a six-bead round rope. It is advisable to string more than you think you will need.

To learn the technique, string 20 in (50 cm) of 6° beads onto a size 10 mercerized crochet cotton. String them in a sequence of six different colors, repeating the sequence. When you crochet the rope, each bead will line up above a bead of the same color, making it easier for you to understand the process. Use a bamboo skewer as a mandrel.

tip
It is much easier to begin working a crochet rope on a mandrel such as a pencil or bamboo skewer. The rope can be removed once the work is under way.

bead requirements for rope lengths

Seed bead size	Length of beads strung on yarn	Length of six-bead crochet rope
6°	5 in (12.5 cm)	1 in (2.5 cm)
8°	5⅝ in (14 cm)	1 in (2.5 cm)
11°	6 in (15 cm)	1 in (2.5 cm)

a simple crochet rope

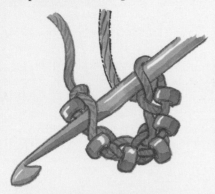

1 Chain six stitches with beads as described on page 162. Flip the chain around and position it as shown in the illustration. Insert the hook into the loop that holds the first bead crocheted. Do not pierce the thread with the hook, or put the hook through the hole in the bead.

2 Bring the new bead down the thread until it nestles against the bead you just passed under the hook. The thread that carries the beads must be positioned to the right of the bead you just passed over the hook.

3 Wrap the thread from back to front over the hook and position it so it can be caught in the hook. Pull the wrapped thread through both loops.

4 Continue working in a spiral until you have reached the length required. As each sequence is completed the beads will change their positions. The beads that have just been stitched will stand in a vertical position whereas beads in previous rows will lie down in a horizontal position.

pattern sequences

By threading shaped or colored beads in
different sequences, many patterns are
possible. These will change, depending on
the number of beads in each round. Since
the ropes are worked in spirals, the repeat
is on the diagonal. You can graph different
possibilities using these charts.

For a crocheted rope with five beads around

For a crocheted rope with six beads around

For a crocheted rope with seven beads around

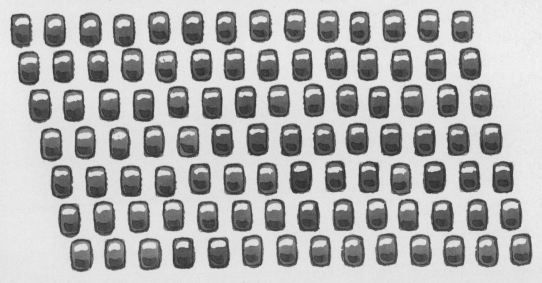

KNOW
YOUR BEADS

This photographic reference chapter will help you to sort your bumpies from your chevrons, your crystals from your glass, and your pearls from your resin. Each listing offers a description of the variations of size, cut, color, and finish possible for each bead. This guide will help you know what you're looking for and show you how to find it.

glass seed beads

Seed beads are usually made from manufactured glass, although occasionally plastic seed beads can be found in the larger sizes (above 8°). Metal seed beads are also sometimes available, including beautiful vintage beads such as steel cuts and newer sterling silver seed beads. Seed beads are used for bead weaving, knitting, and crochet; for stringing jewelry; and providing spacers for larger beads. They come in a wide variety of sizes, shapes, colors, and finishes, which are constantly increasing with new technologies and the growing popularity of beading.

sizes

The size number is indicated by an ° symbol, sometimes written as /0 and pronounced *aught*. The larger the number, the smaller the size of bead. Therefore, an 8° (8/0) is much larger than a 14° (14/0) bead. Below is a list of approximate sizes and weights for the most commonly used beads.

However, different makers list their beads as slightly different sizes. For instance, a Czechoslovakian 11° seed bead will be larger in diameter but with a smaller hole than an 11° Japanese Delica. Two beads of the same size may have radically different-sized holes, which will affect the ease of use when bead weaving. Even within the same make of bead you may find there is a great deal of variation in size and hole.

Generally, Japanese beads are more consistent in their sizing than European beads. While a consistent size may be desirable while weaving, variation in shape and size may give your work a more organic, handmade look. There is no right and wrong choice of beads; it is more a matter of personal choice.

bead sizes and weights

6°	10 beads per 1 in (2.5 cm)	17 beads per 1/16 oz (g)
8°	13 beads per 1 in (2.5 cm)	48 beads per 1/16 oz (g)
11°	17 beads per 1 in (2.5 cm)	100 beads per 1/16 oz (g)
14°	26 beads per 1 in (2.5 cm)	256 beads per 1/16 oz (g)

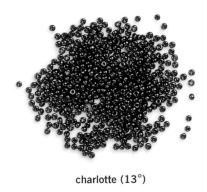

charlotte (13°)

opaque (8°)

tri-cut (15°)

hex cut (8°)

hex cut (11°)

japanese tubes (11°)

finishes

Both seed beads and cylinder beads come in a wide variety of finishes, which greatly influence the final appearance of the beads. They may be transparent, semitransparent, or opaque. Each of these types can be colored or clear.

Colored lining In some cases, a transparent clear glass bead will have a colored lining visible through the outer layer of glass. Vintage green hearts are available with a green core surrounded by a semiopaque glass. The core of the bead can also be lined with a silver or copper foil, which reflects light. These are referred to as silver-lined and copper-lined beads.

Iridescent beads The firing of the glass can cause changes in the appearance of beads. They can take on iridescent effects in many different colors. These include iridescent (sometimes called iris) as well as aurora borealis (often referred to as AB) beads. Beads may also be treated after firing to change the surface appearance to a matte, semi-matte or luster finish.

Galvanized beads These are coated with an unstable zinc-based finish. This coating, which may be shiny or matte, rubs off easily. On the other hand, metal-plated beads have a permanent finish. They are plated with a thin coating of metal, such as high-carat gold, sterling silver, copper, titanium, palladium, or nickel.

Pearl This refers to a lustrous, pearly finish on an opaque bead, while Ceylon refers to a lustrous, pearly finish on a semitransparent bead.

Opal beads Opal beads have a milky semitranslucent finish.

Two-tone beads These are made with two colors of glass and are also available as striped beads made with two or more colors of glass in a striped pattern.

Painted beads Painted or dyed beads have an impermanent color coating. Many bright purples, pinks, and fuchsias are painted or dyed. The color may rub off over time or fade in sunlight.

transparent

opaque

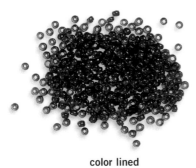

color lined

white heart

silver lined

metallic iridescent

galvanized

opalescent

shape

Although there are variations in the basic seed-bead shape, seed beads come in two main shapes: doughnut and tube.

Rounded (doughnut-shaped) beads are usually referred to as "seed beads" (sometimes called rocaille) and are mainly made in Europe. Charlottes, tri-cuts, hex cuts, and true cuts are all seed beads that have had one or more sides cut off. This provides a subtle sparkle like a gem cut.

Cylinder (tube) beads are less rounded in shape. These are often referred to by their brand names such as Delica or Toho. Cylinder beads are mostly made in Japan. They are not to be confused with longer bugle beads, which are much longer than they are wide. Cylinder beads are about equal in their width and length.

Seed beads and cylinder beads look different when they are woven and each shape has a particular use. A beginner would be wise to select a variety of shapes and sizes since they are often woven in combination with one another.

The pictures below have been enlarged to show the difference in shape between rounded and cylinder beads so are not an accurate represenation of size. Some of the most popular shapes of seed beads are shown on pages 175–177.

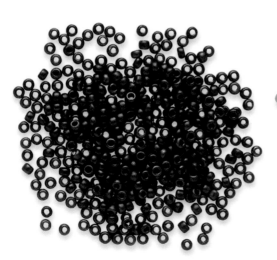

rounded (doughnut-shaped) seed beeds

cylinder (tube) beads

other small beads

The following beads are usually sold alongside seed beads and cylinder beads because they are often worked in with them in weaving and other beading techniques. They come in most of the same finishes as regular seed and cylinder beads.

hex

Hex beads are small six-sided cylinder beads. The cut sides reflect light in a different way from regular, rounded cylinder beads. Their length may be longer than a similarly sized cylinder bead or may be the same size. Check to be sure before combining them in bead weaving. They are available in different sizes and with twists.

cube

Cube-shaped beads are sold in 4 mm lengths which can be substituted in patterns in place of size 6° or 8° beads. They also make good spacer beads for strung necklaces and are interesting when woven together to create large beaded beads.

round

Round glass beads are widely available in a 4 mm width and length. They are useful as a slightly larger bead in bead weaving and other techniques where a 6° bead is called for. They also make excellent spacers on strung jewelry. Sometimes small gemstones can be found and substituted for a 2 mm round.

triangle

Triangle beads have three slightly rounded sides and are available in 5°, 8°, and 10° sizes. They can also be substituted in bead weaving for seed or cylinder beads of a similar size, and their shape will create an unusual contrast in textures within the weaving. They also make excellent spacers on strung jewelry pieces.

tiny teardrops

These small teardrops, about
4 x 6 mm, are often used at the
ends of fringe strands. They can
be used in strung jewelry, but be
aware that they will stick out
more on one side. For this reason
they are usually best strung in
groups where they form
attractive clusters.

tiny tubes

Tiny tube beads are enlarged
versions of the tubular seed
beads. They are 2–4 mm in
length with a large hole. They
look different from bugle beads
because their width is
proportionate to their length;
they do not appear long and
narrow. The large hole makes
them suitable for weaving
patterns that involve many
passes of the thread.

glass beads

Manufactured glass beads are probably the most commonly available beads on the market. They are available in all the same cuts, shapes, and finishes as the seed and cylinder beads listed on pages 170–177, as well as some designs that are only found in these larger sizes. Some additional cuts, shapes, and finishes are listed below. These are the most common and least expensive of glass beads and are often sold in bulk, which are a good value. They are used for strung jewelry and occasionally accents in bead weaving.

sizes

Manufactured glass beads range in size from the tiniest seed beads (about 24°, smaller for vintage ones) up to 20 mm wide. Common sizes rise in increments of 1 mm from 4–20 mm in diameter. The mm size listed next to beads refers to their diameter. Longer beads will often include a length size as well. Glass beads larger than 20 mm are very heavy and are more common among handmade glass beads.

bead styles

The examples on the following pages are styles that are available in manufactured beads. Many of these cuts and shapes are also available in precious and semiprecious stones, pearls, and handmade glass beads. A great number of combinations of finishes make these glass beads appear to be available in many varieties.

melon

This shape is so-called because it has rounded ridges that give it the appearance of a squash or melon. The bead is made as a sphere and then pressed with a straight-edge tool to make the dips. This shape is more common among the handmade beads, but can be manufactured from molds. Some examples have a twist. They can be very round or more oval in shape.

crackle

The insides of crackle beads are shattered, while the outside and the hole are reheated and smoothed. The tiny cracks reflect the light. These are available in round transparent and colored beads in a variety of sizes. They are often made of more than one color.

crow and pony beads

Crow (or roller) beads are named after the Indian tribe that made beautiful beadwork from them. They are usually about 4 mm in diameter and cylindrical with a large hole. They are also available in plastic. Pony beads are similar to crow beads in their outer shape but have a smaller hole and slightly rounder exterior. They are also available in plastic.

glass pearls

Glass pearls are of a better quality than plastic beads with a pearl coating. They are available in a large number of sizes. Although mostly round in shape, drops, pillows, dimpled shapes, rondelles, and a few other shapes are sometimes made. They are available in a wider range of colors than real pearls. The best quality glass pearls are made from lead crystal.

tubes

Glass bead tubes have the hole running through the length and are available in many sizes and finishes. These resemble large bugles. The example on the right is made of different colors of glass to create stripes.

teardrop or drops

Teardrop beads come in different sizes. They have a hole drilled horizontally through the top tip and are often used at the end of a strand of fringe or a dangle. They can be used in strung jewelry, but be aware that they will stick out more on one side. For this reason they are usually best strung in groups where they form attractive clusters.

faceted

Faceted beads are those that have tiny crisp-cut facets on their surface. These reflect light in many directions, creating a sparkle—although not as sparkly as faceted crystal. They are available in a variety of colors, opacities, shapes, and sizes and with many of the same finishes as the seed beads, so it is possible to have a faceted, round, AB finish, 12 mm bead.

striped

Striped beads are made using two or more colors of glass to create stripes. They range from very tiny seed beads to those up to 20 mm. The examples shown on the right are shaped like doughnut beads but are larger than a size 6° at about 5 mm.

rondelle or spacers

Rondelles have a flattened round shape with the hole running through the center lengthwise. They can make a good spacer bead and are available in many colors and sizes. The examples on the right are also faceted.

pear

Pear-shaped beads are flattened spheres in a pear shape. They can have the hole running horizontally across the top end or vertically through the middle as in the example on the right. The example also has a combed pattern in three colors, referred to as a feather pattern.

oval or egglette

Oval-shaped beads are very
popular. They are available in a
wide variety of sizes along with
variations such as pinched, flat,
twisted, and elongated shapes.
They provide a pretty contrast to
the more common round shape.

color-lined

Color-lined glass beads have a
core made of one or more colors
of glass encased in a clear coating.
This style is available in sizes
ranging from tiny seed beads to
the largest glass focal bead. Some
of the examples on the right
include lining in two colors and
raised white stripes on the outside
of the bead as well.

cube

Cube-shaped beads come in many sizes from 2.2 mm to large artist-made beads. The hole can travel through the center from one end to another or diagonally. Flattened cubes are also common in the tablet category. Cube beads usually have slightly rounded corners unless they are faceted.

picasso

Picasso beads have a goldstone marbling or mottling; that is, they have streaks of gold running randomly through them. They are opaque, which makes them appear more like ceramic than glass. Their colors are a bit unusual: "white" has a strong pink tone, "brown" is a mustard-gold, "yellow" is in fact greenish, "red" is almost orange, and "pink" is salmon. The white fades in sunlight, becoming whiter with time.

pressed glass

Pressed-glass beads are most commonly made in the Czech Republic and Germany. Because the beads are pressed in a mold, they can be made in many shapes and sizes. Many of the styles mentioned on the preceding pages, such as color-lined beads, also come in pressed-glass varieties. Below are some of the more novel pressed-glass shapes. These beads are less expensive than artist-crafted beads. They can be bought in bulk and are a good investment for the beginner beader. Shapes like bow ties and leaves have a myriad of uses in all kinds of woven and strung jewelry.

animals

A variety of animal shapes can be found. Common examples include cats, fish, owls, and ladybugs. The fish to the right have an AB finish. Finishes such as these are usually only applied to one side of the bead.

flat flowers

One common type of pressed-glass flower is flat or slightly cupped and has a hole running through the center. These beads are attached like sequins, with a small bead in the middle holding the flower in place.

bow ties

It is often possible to tell if a bead has been made in a mold because there is a small seam line in the glass along the edge of the bead. These bow-tie shapes are pressed glass, but a seam wouldn't show in the narrow edge of the bow tie.

ridged bicone

Shapes such as bicones, cubes, and triangles are often made using the pressed-glass method. Using a mold to make the shapes allows the manufacturer to include extra details, such as the raised ridges of the example on the right.

striped tubes

These striped tubes are another example of the unusual shapes and colorings possible with pressed glass. The beads on the right could have been made with other techniques, but the seam in the banding along the edge gives them away as pressed-glass beads.

vertically drilled leaf

Vertically drilled leaves come in many shapes and sizes. These can either be included in strung beadwork like any other bead, or they can be used individually with a single small seed or cylinder bead at the tip to hold them in place. They make attractive alternatives to drops at the end of fringe strands or hanging from a headpin.

horizontally drilled leaf

Leaves with horizontal holes running across the narrow tip also come in a variety of shapes and sizes. Some are slightly cupped, while others have veining. They can be used in many of the same ways as top-drilled teardrops, hanging from the bottom of a fringe strand.

fruit

Fruit and, less commonly, vegetables can be bought as pressed-glass shapes. The hole can run vertically through the fruit or horizontally through the top end, as in the examples of grape clusters and strawberries on the right.

hearts

Hearts are another popular shape. Pressed-glass hearts usually have the hole running vertically. They can be strung or attached individually with a single seed or cylinder bead at the tip. All pressed-glass shapes will have slightly rounded angles, as in these hearts. For sharp points, you would need to find a faceted or cut heart shape.

handmade glass beads

The beads in this section are made by individual artists working with a flame torch and kiln. Because these beads are made by hand they are usually more expensive than manufactured glass beads. They will all have larger holes than manufactured beads since they are constructed around a mandrel. Check to make sure the hole size is compatible between different beads when selecting the method of stringing or weaving.

shape, cut, and finish

While most handmade beads are extremely well crafted and beautiful, some are made very quickly in small-industry production in India and China. These are not usually as well made or special as a professional artist's bead but are much less expensive. When buying handmade beads, look for a clean bead hole and a smooth doughnut shape (unless they are meant to be a different shape). If the beads have raised bumps, they should be wider at the base, narrowing to the top. Any of the shapes, finishes, and cuts found in seed and glass beads can also be found in handmade beads as well as many more variations and patterns.

Focal beads Many beaders use a handmade artist's bead as a focal bead surrounded with other types of glass, stone, and metal beads. This is because a lot of artist's beads are larger, heavier, more intricate, and more expensive than other beads. A focal bead is usually worn at the front of a necklace. Focal beads come in a wide variety of patterns, from abstract designs to faces, animals, fruit, and other possibilities.

Millefiori The term *millefiori* (also sometimes referred to as murrini, mosaic, or murano) is a combination of the Italian words *mille* (thousand) and *fiori* (flowers). The technique involves the production of glass canes or rods, known as murrine, with multicolored patterns, which are viewable only from the cut ends of the cane. Millefiori beads have plain glass cores. Thin slices of cut cane (murrine) are pressed onto the bead surface while the glass is still hot, forming mosaiclike patterns. Millefiori beads can be decorated sparingly with a small number of murrine, or they can be covered entirely, either by the same style of murrine or by a combination of two or more styles. The murrine can be applied to form a flush, smooth surface or left protruding from the bead. Millefiori beads are impossible to make in a factory and are made by artists all over the world.

Carved glass Carved glass is an unusual technique in bead making. It starts with a rather large, colored-glass bead. The outer layer of colored glass is cut back with engraving tools to reveal an inner core of white or another color of glass.

lampwork bumpies or dots

These are beads with one or more colored raised dots. Check to make sure the dots won't break off. If the bump is narrower at the base than the top, it is not well made. The bumps may be made in transparent, opaque, or combinations of these glasses.

mosaic

These beads have small murrine designs (see page 191) on the surface of the glass. These murrine can be raised or melted into the bead's surface. The example on the right has several different murrine melted into the surface along with dots of different colors.

foil lined

These beads are either completely lined or decorated with small segments of silver, gold, or copper foils. The foil not only looks like trapped metal but also provides an interesting "crackle" texture.

confetti

Confetti beads are rolled in small bits of glass of different colors while the bead is still hot. The beads are not heated any further so the confetti does not melt flush but protrudes from the bead. These can break off if the bead is not well made. Check to make sure the confetti has no undercuts (smaller at the bases than at the top).

hand decorated

Hand-decorated beads cover a wide variety of surface decorations, from bumps to swirls to rosettes. These decorations are not melted flush with the bead but are left as raised decoration. The beads on the right include a variety of bumps.

two-tone

Two-tone beads feature two or more colors in banded stripes. The example on the right includes three different colors as well as opaque and transparent glasses.

raised and inlaid decoration

Glass of a different color is applied to the surface of the bead to create decorative raised patterns. Or, if it is melted further, it creates inlaid decoration. The beads on the right have inlaid stripes that have then been further decorated with blue and white raised dots.

lampworked shapes

Many other shapes of handmade beads are made in production lampwork, including these animals on the right. These novel lampworked shapes should be checked to make sure they will hold up to wear and tear.

artist-crafted glass beads

These individually crafted beads are infinite in their variation. They will usually exhibit a higher level of finish compared to the small production or amateur versions, but will be more expensive. There is also a greater range of colors and finishes.

bumpies and beads with raised decoration

A wide variety of bumpies exists amongst artist-crafted beads. These include beads with extremely intricate dots, and dots within dots. The beads on the right are antiques crafted from opaque glasses.

flat cubes

Great ranges of shapes are possible with handmade beads, including pillows (slightly puffed flat beads) and flat cubes like these, which have been pressed while still warm to create a flattened shape.

focal bead

Individually made examples of these beads will usually be much more colorful and three-dimensional than their pressed-glass cousins. A focal bead is usually heavier and larger than other beads, allowing the bead artist more opportunity to explore her "canvas." The bead on the right is made of borosilicate glass by American artist Nancy Tobey.

foil lined

Various metallic foils can be used inside a clear and transparent glass casing to create unusual and dramatic effects in handmade beads. In this example the silver foil peaks through the tops of the beads, where it is encased in clear glass and is also visible behind the transparent blue glass stripes in the middle of the bead.

millefiori

The tiny mosaic canes used to create the flowers in these beads are typical of millefiori beads. Here the cane flowers are laid into a yellow glass and shaped into a pillow bead.

dichroic

Dichroic glass absorbs light in varying degrees. The term came about because of early observations of the effect in crystals such as tourmaline. In these crystals, the strength of the dichroic effect varies strongly with the wavelength of the light, making them appear to be different colors. These colors can appear to change, depending on the viewer's position and the available light. Dichroic glass appears to glow from within.

borosilicate or boro

Borosilicate glass is a particular type of glass, better known under the brand name Pyrex. It has a very high melting point and produces unique effects when worked with a torch lamp. Unusual colors and shapes are captured beneath a layer of clear borosilicate. As well as the unique colors and markings, boro beads can also feature bumps and other three-dimensional shapes.

flat spots

Raised decoration can be further melted to create flush or inlaid patterns such as these spots. The example on the right shows a pair of antique beads made for the African market.

antique ethnic or trade beads

Trade beads (sometimes called slave beads) are decorative glass beads used between the 16th and 20th centuries as a currency to exchange for goods, services, and slaves. Designed to ease the passage of European explorers and then traders mainly across the African continent, the beads were made throughout Europe, although the Venetians dominated production. Trade beads are also found in the United States and Canada and throughout Latin America. Many very beautiful and collectible beads fall into this category. In some cases, contemporary versions of old trade beads are still made, but some are only available as antiques.

millefiori trade beads

A millefiori trade bead is usually made in a curved, tube shape. They are made with cane ends (see page 203) melted flush into the bead and are almost always made of opaque glasses that have a matte or semimatte surface.

wedding beads

These distinctive beads are usually brightly colored or striped. They have a pear shape with the hole running horizontally across the narrow end. They also come in a flattened variety. They are usually vintage beads made in the Czech Republic with molds.

bottle glass

Recycled bottle glass is used to make crude, organic shapes. The color range is limited: typically blue, green, red, or clear. These beads are usually translucent or almost transparent and have a matte surface. They are still widely made today.

powder glass

This term is sometimes used to describe handmade recycled glass beads, because the glass is ground into a fine powder during production. These beads often come with some unusual markings. The glass is very dense compared to most glass beads. The shapes are organic rounded tubes.

sand cast

Some powder beads are known as sand-cast beads. They have a sandlike, opaque, grainy, matte appearance. They are made in kilns from ground-up recycled glass, often using molds, rather than working them on a mandrel.

chevrons

Chevrons, also called Rosetta or star beads, were first made in Venice and Murano, Italy, at the end of the 14th century. Venetian chevrons are drawn beads, made from glass canes, created in specially constructed star molds. Small quantities of chevrons are still made by artists in Venice and the United States today. Less-expensive versions are produced in China and India.

kiffa

Antique Kiffa beads are among the most valuable beads ever made. They are powder glass beads thought to have resulted from makers trying to mimic the appearance of millefiori beads. They usually come in triangular or pear shapes with the hole running horizontally through the top end. Round ones can also be found. Recent copies are less valuable but also very beautiful.

brass

Brass beads come in yellow-gold and silver colors and are sometimes plated with silver. They are available with a natural patina and in tarnish-resistant varieties. The brass can be engraved with designs as in the examples here, which are worked with wire decoration.

amber

Amber is the ancient resin of trees. The resin has gone through a number of changes over millions of years, the result of which is an exceptional gem that is considered valuable by many cultures. Antique amber beads have a unique patina from many years of use. The examples here are capped with engraved sterling silver.

coconut shell

Coconut-shell beads come in a wide variety of dyed and natural colors. They can be bought in a number of organic and carved shapes. Their natural appearance includes striations and flecks of lighter colors.

bone

Many new and antique examples exist of bone beads. The bones used are typically bovine. Bone is often carved into unusual shapes or etched with designs. Bone beads can be dyed, blackened, bleached, antiqued, or inlaid with other materials, such as shell.

crystals

Crystal is a form of glass with a high lead content. This makes it more expensive to produce than regular glass. It is sometimes referred to as lead crystal. The chemical composition makes the glass optically clearer than other types of glass. Most crystal beads are faceted to take advantage of this property. Different colors are seen in crystal beads because the light is refracted at different angles as it enters and leaves the bead through varying thicknesses of glass; the bead splits the light in the same way a prism does.

quality

There are several qualities of crystal available; higher grades have a higher lead content. Brand-name crystal makers cut glass with computer-controlled precision machinery, which makes very accurate cuts resulting in sparkling crystals. However, hand-cut high-lead crystals are still among the most valuable crystal beads. You should not see bubbles inside good-quality crystal beads.

size

Crystals are available in sizes between 3 mm and 14 mm, with more variety in the smaller sizes. A little crystal goes a long way. Larger pendants are also available.

cubes

Crystal cubes are available with holes running straight through the center or diagonally through the middle. They come in sizes of 4–10 mm in a variety of colors and finishes.

hearts

Heart-shaped crystals usually have the hole running through the top middle. They are used as pendants. Smaller crystal shapes may also be available with a hole running from top to bottom.

chandelier

Chandelier crystals are also
available in a miniature size,
suitable for jewelry making.
Chandelier crystals are named
after the larger ones used in
beautiful sparkling lighting.
These examples are about
12 mm in length.

butterfly

This faceted butterfly is an
example of one of the many
novelty shapes available in
crystal. These are commonly
available in sizes of 6–10 mm in
a variety of colors and finishes.

flower

Crystals come in a variety of
flower shapes. These are available
in sizes of 6–12 mm. These flower
shapes can also be used as
spacers and are backed with
silver to create a rainbow effect
when seen from above. They
would most commonly be used
in jewelry like sequins, with a
tiny bead to hold them in place.

rondelles

Rondelles are flattened, round
beads. They are frequently used
as spacer beads between other,
larger shapes.

faceted nuggets

A faceted nugget is an irregular-shaped bead with facets. The beads on the right are intended to look a little like cut semiprecious stones, with their irregular shape.

multifaceted

Crystals cut with many facets are those most commonly available. These are often in round and bicone shapes, in sizes ranging from 3–14 mm. The facets are usually cut as triangles or hexagons.

pear drops

Drop crystals can be any shape, with the hole running horizontally through one tip. Pear drops have a rounded pear shape and are usually faceted. They may also be referred to as pineapple drops, although pineapple drops are usually less flattened in shape than pears. They come in a wide variety of sizes and make a pretty earring drop.

briolette drop

Briolette drops are similar to pear drops but are elongated and rounder. They come in a wide variety of sizes and work well as earring drops.

metal beads

A wide variety of metal beads are available and can make beadwork resemble jewelry made by a metalsmith. Size, shapes, cuts, and ornamentation vary with each type of metal. Metal beads tend to be hollow to save money on precious materials and to make them lighter. This can make them difficult to thread because the end of the stringing material can catch inside the bead rather than going through the hole. If possible, use a stiff needle rather than a flexible beading needle. The holes of metal beads can be sharp, so select your beading material carefully.

precious metals

Beads are available in all kinds of precious metals, including gold and silver. While they are very expensive, they are well worth the cost if you are creating a special piece of jewelry. Gold- and silver-plated beads can be used to create the effect of precious materials without the cost.

base metals

Some base-metal beads are composed mainly of one single metal, such as brass, copper, or aluminum; others are standard alloys, which are mixtures of different metals. The majority of base-metal beads come in silver, gold, and sometimes copper colors. These can be antiqued to dull and darken the material.

silver

Most real silver beads are sterling silver, which means they are 92.5% pure silver. Silver with a higher purity can be too soft for making beads, unless the bead is a solid, simple shape. Tiny 2 mm silver beads can be combined with glass seed beads in bead weaving to great effect. Silver spacer beads are very popular, as are larger silver beads, which make great focal points. Silver can be cast, engraved, and faceted. Many of the silver beads available on the market are made in Thailand, Indonesia, and India.

thai or hill tribe silver

This has a rustic look that emphasizes an earthy aesthetic. Though simple and a bit rough around the edges, these beads have a compelling presence. They are made of fine silver, which has a higher silver content than sterling silver.

bali silver

Although the Balinese traditionally wear only high-carat gold jewelry, in the 1970s they began to work in silver for the export market and quickly achieved a global reputation for intricate designs in granulation and wirework. A Bali bead is a handmade, sterling silver bead from Bali, Indonesia.

gold

Pure gold is 24 carat and is too
soft for making beads. Nine-
to 14-carat gold is a more
appropriate material for gold
beads. Nine-carat gold refers to
a metal that is nine parts gold
and 15 parts other metals. Nine-
carat gold beads are available
in a variety of sizes and shapes.
Granulated, wireworked, faceted,
cast, and engraved gold beads are
all available.

copper pendant

Gold-filled beads are made from
a base metal, usually brass or
copper, with a sheet of gold
bonded to the surface. This limits
the use of the precious material
to the area where it will be seen.
A bead described as "14k $1/20$
gold-filled" means that the
covering is made from 14-carat
gold, and the total weight of gold
is one-twentieth of the total
weight of the bead.

brass

Brass beads come in a variety of shapes and sizes and several different colors. A common brass bead is the heishi, which makes an excellent spacer. Brass comes in a bright yellow-gold, dull gold, and silver colors. It can also be treated so that it won't tarnish.

copper

Copper can be cast to create many interesting shapes. It can also be antiqued to change the color on all or some areas of the bead. This is often used in combination with relief patterns. It can be faceted as well as engraved. Copper beads are also available cast in a wide variety of shapes and charms.

wire filigree

Wire filigree is made by soldering wire into openwork patterns. It is used to make beads, spacers, and findings and to decorate other metal and cloisonné beads. Wire filigree is a common method of production for many ethnic and antique examples of jewelry.

mixed metal

Many less-expensive but attractive beads are made from amalgams of different metals, such as tin, pewter, and other alloys. These can include hammered, wire filigree, and many other decorative patterns.

cloisonné

Cloisonné is an enameling technique in which the spaces between thin wire partitions (called cloisons) are filled with enamel. The base material is usually copper. First, delicate strips of copper wire are bent to create a design. These are soldered onto the surface of the bead. Next, the spaces between the copper wires are filled with enamels of different colors. Finally, the bead is fired and polished several times.

wire spikes on cloisonné

Many beautiful beads decorated with cloisonné also have raised wire filigree and granulation decorating their surface. Check to be sure the hole is not rough, because it could break threads and wires if the bead is not well made.

semiprecious stones

The stones on the following pages are known as semiprecious or gemstones and can be found with drilled holes for beading. Hole size can vary a great deal in semiprecious beads. Check to make sure the hole size is compatible between different beads when selecting the method of stringing or weaving.

shape and cut

Many of the shapes and cuts described for different types of beads are also available in gemstones. There are also a few additional shapes that can be created because of the hard nature of some stones. For instance, you can find some beautiful carving in gemstones that would not be possible in glass. As well as surface carving on semiprecious stones, many are carved into shapes such as flowers and leaves. These are usually set into metal to be worn as jewelry.

Jade, in particular, has many beautiful, intricately carved examples. These can come from artists all over the world, but the Chinese are well known for making excellent examples.

Shapes with large holes in the center, known as doughnuts, are also more common in semiprecious stones. Doughnuts can come in a number of shape variations, including triangles and half doughnuts.

precious stones

Precious stones such as rubies, emeralds and diamonds are rarely drilled with holes. Since they are so valuable, this would be a waste of material. They are usually set in precious metal rather than beaded.

chinese turquoise

Turquoise is an opaque blue-green mineral that has been prized for thousands of years. It ranges from white to sky blue and from blue-green to yellowish green, often with darker, spidery veining. It is mined in the Americas as well as China and can be bought in many shapes, from unrefined nuggets to highly detailed carvings and faceted stones and beads.

soo chow jade

Jade is most commonly emerald green but also comes in dark and light mottled greens and white, and the rarer colors of yellow, pink, purple, and black. Antique and aged jade comes in a variety of leathery browns and blacks. Jade has been used for ornamentation and making tools since the Stone Age and is found in many parts of the world.

carved jade

Because of its smooth, even texture, jade has long been a preferred material for carving and is often cut into cabochons and pendants for jewelry or other ornaments. Some of these can be very heavy. Antique examples are not uncommon, but often newer jades have been given an "antique" patina to look ancient.

malachite

Malachite is a popular stone with light and dark green banded areas. It can be found in Africa, Europe, and in South and North America. It is often made into cabochons for use in jewelry. Malachite is also available as chips, nuggets, and in carved and faceted shapes as well as round beads.

amazonite

Amazonite is a semiopaque stone of bright verdigris green to bluish green, often with striations of iridescent crystals. It is found in North America, Brazil, Zimbabwe, Russia, Australia, and Namibia. These are available as chips, nuggets, and in carved and faceted shapes as well as round beads.

chalcedony

Chalcedony, found worldwide, is the name for a group of stones made of quartz crystals, which are too small to be seen without high magnification. In jewelry usage, the name chalcedony is usually applied only to the light blue translucent and waxy form shown here.

lapis

Lapis lazuli is a strong blue, sometimes with a hint of violet. Its value decreases with the presence of white patches, while small veins of pyrite are often prized. It has been used as ornamentation since ancient times, and remarkable examples can be seen in collections from ancient Eygpt. Top-quality lapis lazuli comes from Afghanistan, but it is also found in Siberia, Chile, North America, and Pakistan.

aquamarine

Aquamarine stones are transparent and range from very pale blue to blue-green or teal. The most prized color is a deep aqua blue. They can be heat-treated to change their color and improve clarity. The most valuable come from Brazil, but it is also mined in Kenya and Nigeria, Madagascar, Zambia, Tanzania, Sri Lanka, Pakistan, Afghanistan, and Russia.

dyed sea bamboo

Coral is a natural organic substance that has been considered precious since prehistoric times. Coral reefs are endangered, so regulations have been placed on the harvesting and importing of natural coral. Coral occurs in lavender, black, blue, white, and every shade of red. Sea bamboo or bamboo coral is dyed to imitate the fine colors found in natural coral and is often sold in the market today as red coral.

hematite

Hematite is a very common mineral, ranging from steel gray to almost black (specular hematite), brown to reddish brown or red. It is mined in Australia, Brazil (rainbow variety), England, Mexico, and North America. Hematite beads are available in many interesting shapes, including stars and hearts, as well as standard bead shapes and faceted versions.

cape amethyst

Amethyst is a purple quartz, which can display a range of shades, including deep purple, light lilac, lavender, and mauve. Top-quality amethyst is a deep medium purple with rose-colored flashes. Most amethysts on the market today are heat-treated to produce a deeper color. Heat-treating is permanent and these stones will not fade over time.

rose quartz

Rose quartz is another type of quartz, with a pale pink to rose red hue. It is cloudy and often made into faceted beads, such as this drop, to better show off its delicate pink color. Rose quartz is available in chips, nuggets, and in carved and faceted shapes as well as round beads.

scenery jasper

Jasper is an opaque, fine-grained variety of chalcedony. It is found in all colors, including red, brown, pink, yellow, green, gray/white, and shades of blue and purple. It often contains organic material and mineral oxides, which give it interesting patterns, bands, and colors. Many of these patterns resemble landscapes with mountains and valleys, hence the name. Jasper is found worldwide.

ocean jasper

Ocean jasper is a recently discovered type of jasper. It has a wide range of colors, including white, green, gold, peach, pink, and red, and many fascinating orbicular patterns. It is found off the coast of Madagascar.

labradorite

Labradorite is a translucent
feldspar, which displays strong
iridescence when viewed from
different angles. On first glance
it may appear gray, but closer
inspection reveals vivid colors
of bright aqua, golden yellow,
peacock blue, reddish orange,
greens, and red. The best is found
in Finland, but it also comes from
India, Madagascar, Russia, and
Newfoundland.

black onyx

Onyx is a chalcedony quartz mined
in Brazil, India, California, and
Uruguay. It has a fine texture and
black color. Originally, most
chalcedonies, from white to dark
brown and black, were called onyx.
Today we often preface the word
onyx with *black* to distinguish it
from other varieties of onyx that
come in white, reddish brown,
brown, and banded.

carnelian

Carnelian is a member of the quartz family. It has a distinctive reddish brown color that varies in clarity; sometimes it has striations. It is a very hard stone, making it excellent for carving and faceting. Carnelian is available as chips, nuggets, and in carved and faceted shapes as well as round beads.

rhodonite

Rhodonite is a hard, translucent mineral with a distinctive rose pink color. It sometimes exhibits attractive black striations. It is available as chips, nuggets, and in carved and faceted shapes as well as round beads.

pearls

Pearls are available in many colors, shapes and qualities. The unique luster of pearls depends upon the reflection and refraction of light from the translucent layers and becomes finer as the layers become thinner and more numerous. Higher grades of pearl have more layers of nacre (mother-of-pearl). The iridescence of some pearls is caused by the overlapping of successive layers, which breaks up light falling on the surface.

cultured and freshwater

Today, most pearls are cultured, which means that humans have introduced an irritant into the oyster's shell to make it produce nacre in the shape of a pearl. Beads of different shapes are used as irritants, and these result in the different pearl shapes that are available.

Freshwater pearls, on the other hand, form naturally in the oyster's shell and are collected by hunting.

color

Pearls are usually white, sometimes with a creamy or pinkish tinge, but may be tinted with yellow, green, blue, brown, purple, or black. Natural black pearls, frequently referred to as black Tahitian pearls, are highly valued because of their rarity. Color-treated pearls can appear in neutral shades, such as silver, cream and brown, or outlandish colors, such as pistachio, peacock, and lavender.

size and cut

The largest freshwater pearl ever discovered weighed 14 lbs (6.36 kg). Pearl beads come in a great range of sizes from tiny 2 mm rice shapes, increasing up to about 20 mm in diameter. However, there are many unusual, organic shapes, which are best described by their length rather than diameter, such as stick pearls and diamond shapes.

Cultured pearls also come in a variety of shapes, including stars and diamonds. Pearls can be cut with facets to reflect light. Generally pearl beads have very small holes. A bead reamer can be used to increase the size of the hole slightly if it is difficult to work with.

rice

faceted

large potato

stick

dyed

small potato

other natural materials

Many natural materials can be used as beads; some occur naturally with holes, while others need to be drilled. Antique examples can be found as well as newer versions and some that can be made at home. Many of these materials are suitable for carving, dyeing, and painting or can be enjoyed in their natural states.

shell

Shells have an ancient history as beads and ornaments. Some shells occur with natural holes, and many have unique and very attractive patterns. A great variety of natural and carved shells are used as beads and pendants.

bone

Bone is also an ancient material still in use today. It is particularly good for carving and often has a darker color rubbed into its creases to bring out the relief. Bone can be dyed, blackened, bleached, antiqued, or inlaid with other materials, such as shell.

wood

Wooden beads come in a wide range of finishes and can be plain, dyed, painted, inlaid with other materials, such as shell or stones, and carved.

seeds and nuts

A wide variety of seeds and nuts have been used over the centuries for human ornamentation. Some of these are carved and colored before use, others left plain.

other materials

As well as the many unusual natural beads, there are some surprising man-made materials being turned into beads. These can include such objects as pencils, toothbrushes, and junk materials with drilled holes. More commonly though, new and vintage plastics make excellent and unusual beads, as do traditional clays and lacquering methods.

plastic

Plastic beads are often considered the poor relatives of glass beads. However, they should not be overlooked by the serious jewelry maker because they include some beautiful, often expensive, handcrafted polymer-clay artist's beads and vintage plastics, such as Bakelite. Plastic beads are also much lighter than glass beads and are therefore worth considering when weight is an issue.

miracle beads

Miracle beads are made in Japan and are essentially plastic beads. They are referred to as miracle beads or wonder beads because they look as if there is a bead inside the bead. This inside bead is sprayed repeatedly with a reflective material, then given a clear outside coating to achieve the effect.

polymer clay

Polymer is a plastic clay that must be baked in an oven to fire it. It comes in many colors and can be used at home to make beads without the need for a kiln (see pages 58–59). Polymer-clay beads can also be bought. Other materials may also be included within polymer-clay beads, such as glass seed beads.

lucite and bakelite

Lucite, like Bakelite (its pricier cousin), is a vintage plastic material. Lucite beads are still readily available in a great variety of sizes, shapes, and colors. Bakelite beads are less common and are subsequently highly prized by Bakelite collectors.

resin

Resin beads are another kind of plastic bead available to the jewelry maker. They are generally considered to be better quality than regular plastic beads and their price reflects this. They come in a wide variety of shapes and colors, which are reminiscent of sea glass, with its smooth, seamless, matte finish. They are usually made in small workshops in the Far East.

mother-of-pearl

Mother-of-pearl is made from the nacre of a pearl. It can be laminated to many different shapes. There is a wide variety of beads available with a mother-of-pearl finish.

ceramic

Ceramic beads are made from clay that has been fired in a kiln. There are several varieties, including porcelain and raku. Porcelain is a type of clay used in pottery and other ceramics. It is very hard and very white. Porcelain beads can be colored with a slip and glaze overlay, a special glaze, or a slip only. Chinese porcelain beads are the most commonly available, but individual artist's porcelain beads are made all over the world.

clay

As well as porcelain beads, there are many other kinds of clay beads. These include an unglazed variety as shown on the right as well as raku beads that come with a metallic glaze from Greece.

BEAD-WEAVING GRAPHS

Many impressive loom and off-loom bead-weaving techniques can be designed. These can include geometric designs as well as realistic pictures. The smaller the beads that are used, the more realistic the design will appear. Round and tubular seed beads come in such large varieties of color that it is possible to chart highly realistic shading. To keep the weaving flat and regular looking, it is best to stick to just one brand of seed bead per weaving.

graphs

The following graphs will allow you to plot designs. Photocopy them in black and white and then use for your design. You may wish to enlarge the graph on a photocopier for easier reading.

square stitch graph for round seed beads

brick stitch graph

two-drop brick stitch graph

peyote stitch graph

two-drop peyote graph

peyote with cylinder beads graph

right-angle weave graph

herringbone weave graph

Square and loom stitch graph for cylinder beads

Three-bead right-angle graph

Seven-bead netting graph

Five-bead netting graph

appendix

crochet hooks

The numbering of crochet hooks varies a lot from manufacturer to manufacturer. Most makers are now labeling by millimeters (mm) but it is possible to see two hooks with the same millimeter label that are clearly different sizes. Some crochet hook makers have changed their sizes over the years. If using an older crochet hook, try to find a needle gauge that will give you the correct size in millimeters.

This chart offers typical equivalent sizes for the most common hooks for making crochet tubes. It also offers typical thread sizes to be used with these hooks.

Millimeter (mm)	U.S. size	Approximate thread size
0.6	16	100
0.7	14	100
0.75	14	80–100
0.85	13	40–80
0.9	13	40–80
1.00	12	30–60
1.05	11	20–40
1.25	10	20
1.30	10	10–20
1.40	9	10
1.50	8	10
1.65	7	10

crochet stitch definitions

chain (ch)
Start with a loop on the hook (to begin a row this would be a slip-stitch loop). Yarn over hook and pull through. (One chain completed.)

slip stitch (sl st)
With hook through initial loop, insert the hook into a foundation chain or a stitch top. Bring the yarn over hook and draw yarn through both the chain (or previous row stitch top) and the loop on the hook. (One slip stitch completed.)

single crochet (sc)
With hook through initial loop, insert the hook into a foundation chain or a stitch top. Bring the yarn over hook and pull through chain or previous row stitch top (2 loops on hook). Yarn over hook again and pull through both loops. (One single crochet stitch has been completed.)

half double crochet (hdc)
With the hook through the initial loop, bring the yarn over hook and insert the hook into a foundation chain or previous-row stitch top. Bring the yarn over hook again and pull yarn through chain or stitch (3 loops on hook). Yarn over hook again and pull through all 3 loops. (One half double crochet stitch has been completed.)

double crochet (dc)
With the hook through the initial loop, bring the yarn over hook, insert hook into foundation chain or previous row stitch top. Bring the yarn over hook and pull yarn through chain or stitch top (3 loops on hook). Yarn over hook and pull through 2 loops. Yarn over hook again and pull through 2 loops again. (One double crochet has been completed.)

index

acknowledgments

publisher credits

Executive Editor: Katy Denny
Editor: Charlotte Macey
Deputy Creative Director: Karen Sawyer
Designer: Janis Utton
Illustrator: Kate Simunek and Box 68
Photographer: Andy Komorowski
Senior Production Controller: Manjit Sihra
Picture Library Manager: Jennifer Veall

The publishers would like to thank the
following organizations for supplying
beads for photography:

Land of Odds
www.landofodds.com
oddsian@landofodds.com

Rishashay Fine Sterling Silver
www.rishashay.com
inquire@rishashay.com

The Bead Shop
www.beadshop.co.uk
sales@beadworks.co.uk

Happy Mango Beads
www.happymangobeads.com
info@happymangobeads.com

picture credits

Special Photography: © Octopus
Publishing Group Limited/Andy
Komorowski

Other Photography: © Octopus Publishing
Group Limited/Graham Atkins-Hughes 1,
4, 6, 12 left, 12-13, 14, 15 top, 15 bottom,
16-17, 18 left, 24 left, 24 right, 25, 26, 28,
29, 30 bottom left, 31 top right, 32, 33, 38,
45, 48, 52, 81, 91, 95, 102, 107, 112, 115,
122, 171, 172-173, 180 top, 181 bottom, 185
top, 197, 206, 216 bottom, 217 bottom, 229,
230-231, 232 top, 233 bottom; /Vanessa
Davies 22, 157; /Sandra Lane 2, 9, 10, 41,
42-43, 63, 68-69, 82, 83, 84, 86-87, 137,
140, 149, 151, 152, 168-169, 170, 178, 194
top, 229 top left, 236-237.